IN MY SKIN

SOPHIE LEE

In My Skin

Learning to love your perfectly imperfect life

First published in Great Britain in 2024

Society for Promoting Christian Knowledge
The Record Hall, 16–16A Baldwins Gardens
London EC1N 7RJ
www.spck.org.uk

British Library Cataloguing-in-Publication Data
A catalogue record for this book is available from the British Library

Hardback ISBN 978-0-281-08940-6
eBook ISBN 978-0-281-08941-3
audio ISBN 978-0-281-08987-1

1 3 5 7 9 10 8 6 4 2

Typeset by Fakenham Prepress Solutions
First printed in Great Britain by Clays Limited
Subsequently digitally printed in Great Britain

eBook by Fakenham Prepress Solutions

Produced on paper from sustainable forests

Contents

Contents

Foreword

There are a lot of loud voices telling us what it means to be a strong woman at the moment. In a world saturated with instructions and advice, Sophie stands firm, demonstrating strength rather than just talking about it.

This is the memoir of a fierce woman. A woman who fiercely defends her cultural roots, is fiercely loyal to her loved ones and is fiercely protective of those who haven't yet found their voice.

I was first introduced to Sophie online; I suppose that's how we connect with most people these days. I came across her story when she started bravely sharing about her life-changing facial injuries on social media. Seeing pictures of her in hospital and reading about her fears, uncertainty and treatment took me back to those days of my early recovery following my own life-changing event.

I messaged her to lend some support – remembering how lonely those first weeks were – and we quickly formed a friendship. Sophie is an encourager of women. She's the cheerleader we all need in our lives – quite literally at times, given her dance training!

Even if you don't have the pleasure of being personally championed by this woman, you can be inspired and encouraged by her journey. I know perhaps more than anyone what it's like to embrace an injury that alters your looks when you've been in an industry that prizes attractiveness over anything else. That was when I truly felt UnSeen, and in these pages you'll hear that Sophie felt the same. But like a phoenix from the ashes, she pieced her world back together and created something even more beautiful.

This isn't simply a story of an accident. This is the story of a life lived to the full despite trolls, critics and even racism. Other people's opinions – some measured and some, as you'll see in this story, laced with hatred – are hard to silence. Publicly, she greets hostility with grace, good humour and just a hint of sass. But I know that behind closed doors, it has been a process of overcoming.

I hope people will read this and feel inspired. My hope is that young people who face bullying in school will see that things do get better. To anyone who is subject to vicious racial slurs, I hope you hear Sophie when she says that it has everything to do with the bullies and nothing to do with you.

As the old proverb goes, it takes a village to raise a child, and it's true that Sophie is the product of several strong people – many of them women – who have supported her. I feel fortunate to have benefited from their wisdom, as well as hers, in reading this book. Hearing about her relationship with her grandparents and the strong bond she has with her mum is touching. I imagine kite sales and karaoke room bookings will increase among readers of her story!

I am so proud that Sophie's book is the second in my imprint, The UnSeen. Stories of overcoming and radical self-acceptance help us all to take a step further towards loving and accepting ourselves. If Sophie can step out with such boldness after facing so many trials, why can't we? I hope that, like me, you will feel moved, entertained and challenged as you read her story. It's time, like Sophie, that we all embraced ourselves and became more comfortable in our skin.

Katie Piper OBE

Prologue

The longest split second

There are plenty of rules in my job, but one of them is that you can't stare at the flames. A quick look is fine, just to make sure everything is as it should be, but you need to trust yourself and your equipment. That's easier said than done, but I do usually manage it, allowing the spectacle to take centre stage without opening my eyes. But this time I just couldn't help it. I couldn't resist.

I was diligent in my checks before the show. You can never be too careful when you're playing with fire. It was a new venue, but everything else was the same. There was no reason for me to be worried, but even so the stakes felt high. I wanted to be sure that the jet of flames was directed at the ideal angle, away from the stage. I wanted the audience to be able to see it dancing into the air in a stunning blaze; the perfect finale to my performance.

Everyone had gasped as I sprayed the paraffin out of my mouth. A crack had ripped through the air as the liquid caught alight. And that was when I peeked, hoping to see the flames in a fiery billow out in front of me. Only they weren't.

Through the gaps I had allowed to form between my eyelids, I saw a fireball launching towards my face. The heat was projecting back towards me, but there was no time to protect myself.

It was the fastest and slowest moment of my life.

The whole thing happened in a split second, but I can still play it through frame by frame. The terrifying sight of the fire hurtling back to me. The scorching feeling on my face. My sharp intake of breath.

As the fire licked over my skin, it clung to the droplets of paraffin that had splattered onto my chest and neck. I knew I had to act fast.

I needed to extinguish the flames before they crawled all the way up my neck to my face. I started to smell the unmistakable odour of burning hair. My heart thumped inside my fiery ribcage.

I was on fire for less than thirty seconds, but that was all it took to scorch my skin, changing my appearance – and my life – forever. I felt dizzy, I felt hot, I felt humiliated. I felt breathless, I felt scared, I felt exposed. I felt exhibited, I felt horrified, I felt alone. And this was just the start.

1
Made in China

I was born in Blackburn, Lancashire. Where I'm from, your chips come with gravy and the only biscuit worth dunking in your cup of tea is a Hobnob. But I haven't always lived around here. Despite spending most of my formative years in the small market town of Darwen, I lived in China until I was four years old, and my first language is Cantonese.

Mum

My mum, Angela, was born on 24 September 1962 in Hong Kong. The region was experiencing extreme drought, and during that first year of her life there were periods when water use was restricted to just four hours over a period of four days. Extended families lived together, with many generations under one roof, and most working-class people toiled for long hours in factories to earn a modest wage. The economy was on the up, but most families – my mother's included – continued to struggle.

My mum grew up in the suburbs, away from the neon lights and high-rises of Hong Kong's bustling cities. Her eldest sister had been adopted from another family in the village, and then came her elder biological sister and brother, so she was the youngest of four children. It wasn't uncommon at the time for baby girls to be cast out by their disappointed parents, most of whom wanted a boy. My grandparents adopted the eldest girl when she was four.

The family home was unstable, and my grandmother went off with another man when my mum was just four years, leaving my grandfather in charge. The eldest sister felt she had no option but to step up and take on some of the parental duties, despite her young

11

age. This obligation became more pronounced when my grand-father sunk into ever-increasing debt and depression as the result of a gambling addiction.

When my mum was seven years old, the family packed up and emigrated to the UK, landing in Manchester's inner-city Moss Side area. Far from the rolling landscapes of rural Hong Kong, she was faced with extreme deprivation in a dark, damp part of town. Moss Side has a long association with drugs, gangs and violence – and in the 70s, when they arrived, it was at the peak of its notoriety.

The four siblings were, for the most part, left to fend for them-selves. Without consistent supervision, Mum leaned on her eldest sister for support and parenting. She had a difficult relationship with her brother, who bullied and taunted her, taking pleasure in the abuse. On one occasion they were all sharing a fish and chip tea when he spat into a tub of curry sauce and tried to force her to eat it. When she refused, he grabbed a broom and whacked her over the head with it until she started bleeding. On another occasion he snuck into her room and set fire to some of her possessions using a lit cigarette. No one was hurt, but her precious childhood bedroom went up in flames.

Having never attended school in Hong Kong or learned any English, turning up at a Moss Side primary school was terrifying for my mum. She and her siblings were the only Chinese pupils at the school, or indeed in the area at all. As she got older, Mum spent more and more time out of the house. When she left school at sixteen, she took three jobs so she could afford to move out and live by herself.

Mum's first job was at the huge printworks factory in the centre of Manchester, back when it was still a printworks and not a vast entertainment complex. At weekends she would serve coffee and iced buns at a local cafe, and in the early mornings she would deliver newspapers.

Dad

One month before my mum's birth, my dad, Lee Yau Quan, was born in a small village called Di So Ham in the south of China.

His name meant 'You've got the power'. We tend to celebrate his birthday on 23 August, but as he still follows the Chinese calendar, we struggle to keep up with the official date as it changes every year.

The youngest in a family of five, my dad's upbringing was very different from my mum's, but did not come without its own hardships. My dad's parents were loving and did their best to be present, but when their fifth child came along, unplanned, they were terrified they wouldn't be able to feed their family. They discussed selling him to a rich couple who could afford to give him a better upbringing, and even found some willing and wealthy recipients. They made their way over to this family's home to hand over the precious little boy into what they hoped would be a better life, but at the last moment, my grandad looked down at him, touched his forehead and decided he couldn't go through with the sale.

While the idea of selling a baby seems unthinkable to us in the Western world, it wasn't uncommon in China at this time, as the realities of life were far harsher than those to which most of us are accustomed. There are horrific stories of newborns being drowned by desperate parents who simply didn't have the money to raise them, so I guess my dad was one of the lucky ones. From that point on, my grandparents did all they could to put food on the table for their family of seven.

In order to do so, both parents were out working all hours, which came at a cost to family time. My grandad was the rice rationer for their village; a job that made him well known and respected in the area. When the children were slightly older he got a new job in the city of Guangzhou, which meant he was away from the family for months at a time. My grandma worked as a seamstress, as well as taking care of the children and the household.

The family grew their own crops and ate the food from the harvest. My dad was enrolled in school, but was often absent. Sometimes he couldn't afford to get there and other times he stayed at home to help with the crops instead. There was always work for him, harvesting the grain or tending to the chickens.

My dad was twenty-four when he moved to the UK. He was convinced there would be better earning opportunities abroad, and he wanted to be able to send money back to his family in China, so he packed a small bag with very few possessions and spent the entirety of his savings on a flight to Liverpool, where he found his first job working in the kitchen of a small restaurant. Initially, with poor English and no experience, he took on the most junior role in the kitchen, washing pots, peeling potatoes and chopping vegetables. In order to fit in, he adopted the British name Paul, which everyone still calls him today. He worked his way up, and as his skills and grasp of the English language improved, so did his job title and pay. He built a reputation as a hardworking and talented chef, and quickly got himself promoted to the coveted position of head chef.

Given that there weren't many Chinese people in the UK during the 1980s, the community tended to stick together, and Dad spent his limited free time with others who had emigrated to the UK from China. It was through this extended network that he met my mum's eldest sister, who was settled in Liverpool by this time. She insisted there was someone Dad should meet, and he reluctantly agreed to be set up on a blind date.

When my mum talks about that time, all she remembers is how kind he was. She says she never met anyone who treated others so well. Neither of them had a lot of money, but Dad found ingenious ways to make Mum feel special without spending a fortune. Using his skills in the kitchen, he once carved a bouquet of roses out of carrots, as he couldn't afford the real thing from the florist.

My dad was courteous and gentlemanly, and Mum noted that, unlike a lot of other Chinese men she knew, he ate quietly. It was such a small thing, but she loved this about him; the way he made no sound while he was chewing. After a year of dating, they got married and decided to relocate to Blackburn.

Their home wasn't plush; it was just a simple two-up two-down terraced house on Lower Cross Street in Darwen. The windows rattled in the wind and the floorboards creaked with every move. The house was cold. Even with the limited central heating turned to maximum, the uncarpeted floors sent a chill from the soles of your feet to the top of your head. The whole block was later demolished to make way for a community academy, which, years down the line, my younger sister would attend.

That shabby home was not only the first place they shared as a married couple, but the first place I ever lived. I was born a year after they moved in together. When Mum found out she was pregnant they were overjoyed, and Dad insisted that she stop working and rest ahead of the birth. But my independent mum couldn't go from her three-job routine to nothing, so she secured some work as a dinner lady at a local school.

While serving in the lunch hall, she came across a sweet Asian girl called Sophie, who was always polite and strikingly beautiful. That's how she picked my name. Born on 1 August 1995 in Blackburn hospital, I was named Sophie Lee in English and Lee Sau Yee in Cantonese. I had a thick mop of black hair, and both parents were besotted at first sight. They vowed they would always provide and give me more than they had ever had as children... but that meant some big sacrifices lay ahead.

2
Child's play

My parents were driven. They had a vision for the life they wanted for themselves and for their family, and were willing to put in the hard work to achieve it. They knew the opportunities were out there, and wanted to make sure their children got the very best. I admire their work ethic, but growing up I didn't understand it. I didn't understand the focus on their jobs and on saving money. I didn't understand why they weren't around more. And most of all, I didn't understand why they sent me to live with my paternal grandparents in China without them.

Once my mum had recovered from the birth and I was no longer being breastfed, my parents decided to open a business. They secured the lease on a takeaway food premises and opened their own chip shop. It was basic fare for Friday night fish night, with big jars of pickled eggs, onions and massive gherkins on the beige countertop. They called it Lee's Cantonese Kitchen. When we think of entrepreneurs today, most of us envisage private jets and internet start-ups. But this was long hours and real toil. It meant staying open after the pubs closed and opening up again in time for lunch. But it was a small slice of Blackburn that was all theirs. They worked hard for it, and they earned their success. Lee's Cantonese Kitchen still stands on the corner of 87 Suddel Road to this day, and twenty-seven years on, my parents are still at the helm.

Their labour paid dividends, but it came at a cost. Aware that they would be needed for long hours in a shop filled with deep-fat fryers, which was therefore no place for a baby, they had a tough decision to make. They couldn't afford to hire anyone else to work in the shop, so they asked my dad's parents if they would take me for a few years while they focused on growing the business.

At the time, I was too young to have any grasp on what was happening. I was nine months old when my parents flew over to China to leave me with my grandparents. Back in that same village in Guangdong where my dad grew up, they took me to meet his parents, who would care for me for the first four years of my life. That's how I ended up in China. We flew over together, and they stayed with me for a week or two to help ease the transition before returning to the UK, leaving me there. I settled, and my grandparents cared for me well.

Despite my parents having been desperate to move to the UK and out of China, I would describe my early years as idyllic. I had free run of the house and the road at the front. Children were allowed to be children. There was no danger in playing in the street because someone – usually my grandma – was always outside. Grandma would sit in a rickety outdoor chair, keeping an eye on the kids or chatting to the neighbours. There were always people around and everyone knew each other.

As I got older, I made a friend of a similar age who lived a few doors down. I would knock for him, and he would come out and play in the street with me. We were allowed to explore and go on adventures. One of our neighbours had a big tree in the front garden. We were obsessed with it. We would strain, jump and, if all else failed, lift each other up to swing on the sturdy branches that hung low over the garden. When one was holding on, the other would push their body like a human swing, and we would shriek as we flung ourselves back and forth. My grandma had warned me once that it was a lucky tree, so we would be in a lot of trouble if we snapped the branch. The mystique only served to make this pastime more appealing.

There was a lot of laughter, a lot of freedom and a lot of food in those early days. Once I moved on to solid foods, I started eating the same meals as my grandparents. Each day started with a breakfast of bao buns. These small, steamed buns are slightly sweeter than dumplings, and are stuffed with fillings such as beef or pickled vegetables. These days they feature on the menus of trendy London eateries, but as a child they were my version of cornflakes.

Sometimes we would have cheung fun, a steamed rice-noodle roll filled with prawns or spring onions. Grandma would also give me milk curd, a sweet, yogurt-like drink to go with my food. I was obsessed with this treat and asked for it all the time. I even made up a song that I sang any time I wanted milk!

We went for two walks every day; one after breakfast and a second after dinner. We would always take the same route around the neighbourhood, me finding anything and everything to touch and play with and climb on, and Grandma and Grandad stopping to chat with people we passed. During the morning walk Grandad would often syphon himself off to join his friends, who would be sitting out playing chess. In the evenings he would carry a kite, and we would fly it together as the sun set.

I had so much energy as a child, and was a complete livewire. I ran around like Donnie – the feral, adopted son from the cartoon *The Wild Thornberrys*. I would constantly tear around the house or street out front immersed in some imaginary game. My enthusiasm made me a joy for my grandparents but also a challenge as they struggled to keep up, but if any grandma was up to the task, mine was.

There were always other family members around. In our culture, families stay close; either in the same house or nearby. Even where I am now in Blackburn, my relatives all live in the same cluster of roads. In China we lived in the same house as my dad's eldest brother and his wife. They were kind, and helped with me from time to time, but they weren't my primary carers. I was raised for those years by my grandma and grandad.

Grandma

From the moment I arrived in China, I built an unshakeable bond with my grandma. She was the one who soothed me when I cried, the one who sat with me as I fell asleep and the one whose bed I would dive into in the mornings. I remember the gentle lullabies and Chinese folk songs she sang to help me doze off. It was the theme tune to a peaceful childhood. I couldn't help but see my grandma as my mother figure. That's what she was. It wasn't unusual in China for older generations to take on the childcare so the younger adults could work, and I certainly wasn't the only one who spent a lot of time under the care of their grandparents.

One of Grandma's prized possessions was a karaoke machine she had bought from a friend at the market. I have stacks of photos of myself standing in front of the machine in the glow of the multi-coloured lights, clutching at a giant microphone. The microphone covered most of my little face, but I didn't care. I just wanted to perform for my grandma.

She was the epitome of eccentric. Kind to everyone she met, she was known and liked by the whole village. But her larger-than-life personality wasn't matched by her 4ft 11 (1.5m) frame. She sported voluminous jet-black curls that protruded from her head with the same structural integrity as a well-groomed afro. I was in awe of her big curly hair, but given that no one else in our family wore the same style, it only occurred to me in adulthood that it must have been the result of regular perming. She kept it short in later life and never allowed greys to poke through, opting for an inky-black box dye to maintain the colour.

She worked as a seamstress, making clothes and dresses to be sold in shops or at the market. Years of hard work had enabled her to perfect her craft, and she could whip me up a sweet little outfit from a selection of offcuts in a couple of hours. This meant I always had something new to wear. These outfits were usually adorned with bows, puffy sleeves or a princess-style skirt. With Grandma, every day was dress-up day. As I got older, I would point out things I liked, and she would make me my own version from old fabric.

I like to think that, in another life, or at another time, my grandma would have been a performer. She was talented at making clothes, but she also had such character and charisma. She would have captivated audiences on any stage. In order to encourage me to appreciate the arts she took me to the Chinese opera and theatre show as a little girl. I'm certain this instilled in me a love of acting and the stage. She would dance around the house and sing to me, repeating the words so I could learn the lyrics and sing along.

Grandma was always kind and patient. I was allowed to be loud and attention-seeking, and sing and shout and jump around, and my spirit was never dampened. I was always encouraged to be lively and be myself. Passion, and expressions of it, were actively encouraged, and many of my personality quirks that could easily have been pushed down were celebrated. I was constantly told to believe in myself and never made to feel as though I couldn't achieve more.

I'm convinced that it was during these early years that I developed my interest in clothes, fashion and the performing arts. I love my grandma for that with every inch of my being, and when I think about those days, I could burst with affection for her.

The two of us were inseparable. While Grandma was playing Mahjong, I was sitting on her lap trying to take it all in and learn how to play for myself. I would watch her shuffle her tiles around and think, *I want to be like that when I'm older.*

As she prepared food, I would be by her side. She would hand me the offcuts of the veggies and let me pretend to cook on the counter next to her. After our morning walk, when Grandad had gone off to play chess, the two of us would head to the market. This was where Grandma's real talents came into play, and she used every tool to her advantage. Whenever a crowd gathered around a particular stall, she would use her below-average height to stealthily slide to the front of the crowd to find out what new deal people were fawning over.

The market we went to wasn't like the modern supermarkets in China or the UK. It was an open market, the stalls stacked high with fresh produce, spices and meat. People set up little shops for themselves by laying a blanket on the ground and piling their wares on top. The market was alive; not just the people within it, but the place itself. It pulsed and breathed with the swell and retreat of the crowd. Everything was loud and brightly coloured, and I would be swept up in the vibrancy of my surroundings. The bustling streets would have been overwhelming if I hadn't been there with Grandma, who held my hand as we navigated the vendors.

When she identified something she wanted, Grandma made sure she got it – and for the price she wanted, too. I remember her haggling over some fresh vegetables once. The vendor put them in the metal bowl suspended under the scales and quoted her a price. She instantly fired back that the water droplets on the skin of the veg would add to the weight, so she would need a discount. Other times she would convince sellers to drop the price if she could see any wilting on the leaves. She was razor-sharp, and always made sure she walked away with a complete shopping list, having paid the lowest possible price.

Grandad

On the surface, my grandma and grandad weren't an obvious match, but when you dug deeper they complemented each other perfectly. They were very young when they got married, having grown up in the same village. While she was larger-than-life, he conveyed a sense of calm. While she loved to put on a show, he would sit on the sidelines and survey the action.

Grandma called him 'Gi Gong', which translates as 'Chicken Man'. It sounds like she was taunting him, but it was her affectionate nickname for a man who loved chickens. He would spend hours outside tending to and caring for the chickens that would eventually become a meal for the family.

Every now and again, Grandad would take me along to one of his chess gatherings. I would stand there, shyly clinging to his legs, and he would encourage me to greet each of his friends. Then I'd sit and watch, marvelling at this complex game that had the grown men stumped for hours at a time.

Despite his advanced years, Grandad remained active. He never stopped moving around, taking on projects and doing jobs around the house. He was somewhere between a DIY expert and a craftsman. To me, it seemed there was nothing he couldn't make or fix. He stood by the traditional value that possessions weren't to be thrown away until absolutely every other solution had been attempted. It didn't matter how battered a toy of mine became, if there was a way to patch it up and prolong its life, that's what he did.

I was once given a second-hand tricycle that I absolutely adored. I would whiz around the garden and down the road on it. I refused to pedal, so I simply push-started myself with my foot, then allowed the wheels to gain momentum. While this was fun for me, the technique put additional strain on the front wheel, and it once came flying off and rolled down the street. After I had collected the errant part, Grandad set about restoring the tricycle to its former glory. I managed to break the bike in many other ways over the following year, and each time I presented him with the fragmented toy, he patiently sat down to put it back together again. On one occasion he returned it to me with a piece of string attached to the handlebars. Knowing I didn't like to pedal, he had attached the new element so he could pull me along and we could play together. From that point on I simply lifted my feet up away from the pedals and he would walk on ahead with the string in his hand.

He also busied himself building kites or restoring old ones for us to take on our afternoon walks after dinner. At one time I was obsessed with manga character Sailor Moon, a pretty blond super-hero with knee-length pigtails and thigh-high boots. Grandad covered an old kite with a picture of her, then attached two long strings comprised of empty ramen packets he had salvaged from a local factory to either side of the kite. They made it look as if her long hair was blowing in the wind. I was in love with it. Grandad had always taught me to be cautious about attaching things to our kites, explaining we needed to make sure they were still light enough to fly, but he often tacked on new things himself or used tape or string to patch up any damage.

If either of my grandparents told me off, I would go straight to the other and cry. It's a tried-and-tested tactic that many would call manipulative, but three-year-old me had no problem playing my grandparents off against each other. My grandma tended to be the softer of the two, but neither was particularly harsh. They had already had their own children, so the second time around they didn't feel the anxiety of new parents. They loved me and showed me all the affection they had to give, which fortunately for me was a lot. I will always be grateful for the childhood they gave me.

Change afoot

My parents came back to visit me as frequently as they could, about once a year. I still remember some of their later visits, and the feeling of distance I had towards them. I knew they were my mum and dad, and that I was living with my grandma and grandad, but I didn't feel the familiarity and comfort I thought I was supposed to. They always brought sweets and toys as gifts when they came over, but it was hard to muster any excitement about their visits when I didn't really know them.

My parents wanted to put me into primary school at the age of four, so I knew I would have to go back to the UK with them. Little did I know how intense the culture shock would be when that day finally came.

3
Back to Britain

Grandma flew back with me to the UK, to help me settle in. My return to England was harder for her than for me, as I didn't understand what we were doing. To me, it was just a trip with my grandma, the woman who had raised and cared for me.

She took me to the house in Darwen where my mum and dad lived, but I hid under the table every time she left me alone with my parents. I just couldn't adjust to the idea of not having my grandma around. I missed her, but as I still spent my summers in China with her and Grandpa, I got to spend extended time with them each year. I remember thinking my mum was loud. She was so much noisier than my grandma and grandpa. It was a real adjustment learning how to be around them after spending most of my life away.

And it wasn't just my caregivers that changed. Everything did. I was used to living in an area that was safe, where there were always people sitting out in the street keeping an eye on the children playing. I had freedom there. But none of that was possible on the grubby streets of Darwen, where the crime rate was high compared with other Lancashire towns. Grandma had taken me to the opera in China, and I visited numerous parades and cultural events. I was surrounded by colour and vibrancy, by spectacular sights and sounds. There was always something to see and experience. But in the UK that stopped. It simply wasn't a part of the lifestyle. Added to that, my parents worked around the clock to provide for me, so they didn't have time for the same activities.

A new home and nursery

Because of the long hours they worked at the restaurant, I didn't move straight back in with Mum and Dad. I initially went to live with my mum's friend, whom I called Auntie Mae. She would give me breakfast and drop me at nursery, then come back to pick me up again. Mum took on the school-run duties when she was able and regularly took me on days out, but that was only once a week at the most. Whenever Mum dropped me back to Auntie Mae's I would cry and run over to the window to watch her leave. I had all my needs provided for, but I still didn't feel as if I had my mum and dad. I couldn't help but feel as though I'd been left behind, and I remember feeling sad.

Over the years I've brought this up with my parents, asking why I wasn't able to live with them, and why they weren't around much. We've even argued about it. I understood that huge sacrifices had to be made to keep a business running, but I understand something now that I didn't back then. When you're an immigrant couple trying to start a business from scratch, and English is your second language, you have to make tough choices to survive. There was no way they could both work until 11 p.m. and care for a preschool-aged child. Just as that sacrifice was hard for me, it was difficult for them. All those hours they put in were to give me the future I dreamed of living.

Auntie Mae's house came complete with two playmates: my older cousins Alfred and Ricky. The boys loved to play football and would wrestle each other – and sometimes me! I got used to their rough-housing and WWE obsession. It was fun growing up with other kids, but it was a very different environment from the dresses and opera of my grandparents' world in China. My cousins still joke that when I first came back to the UK, I was a country bumpkin. I knew nothing about the Western world with its TV shows and cartoon characters. I didn't even speak the language. I had spent all my life up to that point speaking Cantonese, the language from our region, and I even spoke that with a rural village twang.

I started nursery with no English, but quickly adapted to the new language. I managed all right – children learn things quickly.

My parents didn't want me to drop the Cantonese, so I went to Chinese school every Sunday to make sure I continued to improve, and learned to read and write in my mother tongue. I didn't take well to an additional day in class when my friends were enjoying their weekends. As I got a bit older, I started playing up, not doing my homework on time and being cheeky towards the Cantonese teachers.

Mealtimes at Auntie Mae's were always fun, with me and the two rowdy boys jostling for the best bits of each dish set down in the middle of the table. Auntie Mae would serve up plates of rice, delicious crab and all the normal English dishes like shepherd's pie, and bangers and mash. My bedroom at Auntie Mae's was simple. I enjoyed having the space to myself, and there was a window that gave me a view of the back of the house and down the lane that approached the garden. I would sit staring out of it with my head in my hands, daydreaming that my parents would come walking down that lane to take me home with them. Despite seeing them regularly, I missed my parents terribly, especially my mum.

My parents paid for everything for me, from food to school uniforms and toys. I was obsessed with my play cleaning set, which included an iron and a hoover. I would walk around, pushing it across the floor pretending to collect dust and fluff from the carpets. Sadly, my enthusiasm for cleaning hasn't continued into adulthood, but it was a promising start!

My toy box looked like the grid of a nostalgic 1990s Instagram page. I had those squidgy aliens that made your hands smell weird; a slinky I would carefully position at the top of the stairs to make sure it had an uninterrupted descent; and a Tamagotchi, which was often too great a responsibility for me, so my rabbit (or was it a hamster?) frequently died and I would have to reset the gadget. It wasn't the only one of my toys that hassled me for food. I had to take the batteries out of my Furby when it woke me up in the middle of the night demanding: 'Feed me!'

The first character I fell in love with when I got back to the UK was Po, the smallest and cutest of the Teletubbies. The red tubby with her blue-and-pink scooter immediately caught my attention.

I was enthralled watching the show on Saturday mornings. For my fifth birthday, my mum surprised me by coming into nursery with a Po cake. I was kitted out in Teletubby gear from head to toe. I stood on my tiny plastic chair as the cake was brought over with five glowing candles sticking out of it. Everyone sang 'Happy Birthday', and I remember surveying the rest of the class from my slightly elevated vantage point and thinking, for the first time: *I've got friends!*

School and siblings

I soon moved up to primary school and continued to build friendships. I had school dinners with everyone else – I remember eating pizza slices and turkey twizzlers before Jamie Oliver got involved in setting a healthier menu. For pudding we were often served a square sponge bake from a tray, slathered in gloopy yellow custard. I loved the crust and would ask for a corner piece, smiling sweetly at the dinner lady. She always accommodated my request because I reminded her of her own daughter.

I would skip around the playground creating imaginary worlds and playing in them with my friends at break times. We would lie on the grass and make daisy chains that sat on our heads during these games. Once we were playing tig (or tag, or chase or it – depending on what you called it back then), and we dumped all our coats in a big pile on the floor before running around trying to catch each other. One of the 'catchers' had me in their sights and was about to close in on me, so I went straight for the coat mountain and hurled myself over it. Rather than outrunning my pursuer, I ended up crashing headfirst into a stone wall and cracking my head open. I felt the warm blood trickle down my face. I don't remember the pain; I just remember the shock. I burst into tears.

The teachers scooped me up and took me to the first-aid room, where a dinner lady sat with me until my mum arrived. I was so relieved when I saw her walk through the door, as I knew she would look after me. The cut on my head was deep enough that I needed a couple of stitches. Mum bundled me into her

Mitsubishi Shogun and took me to A&E, where they patched me up. Then I got to go home with Mum for the rest of the day and the day after.

I was seven when my parents had their second child, Kelvin, and I struggled to welcome him into the family. I already felt I didn't get enough of my mum and dad's attention, and now there was another person making demands on their time. I was mean to him in subtle ways I hoped my parents wouldn't notice, but of course they did. If Mum told me he needed to sleep, I would pick that moment to play at being in a rock band in the next room, sometimes even collecting pots and pans from the kitchen as my instruments. I was once caught wafting a blanket over him while he was sleeping in an attempt to wake him up. On another occasion I emptied the contents of Mum's purse all over the floor and then solemnly explained that Kelvin had been the perpetrator.

A few months after he arrived, my parents flew out to China with him. He stayed in my grandparents' home and was given the same introduction to our culture as I was.

Just when I thought I had their attention to myself again, my mum had another baby, this time a girl called Siobhan (Shivie for short), eighteen months after giving birth to Kelvin. Shivie wasn't sent to live with my grandparents, as it was the year of the severe acute respiratory syndrome (SARS) outbreak, which originated in China and spread to four other countries. Instead, she moved into Auntie Mae's with me. Shivie developed a closer bond with her than I did, as she grew up there from a very early age. While Auntie Mae became a mother figure for Shivie, I always saw my grandma in that role.

A bitter blow

Despite settling in well at school, the hardships came – some of them perceived and some very real. One of the disappointments I remember most vividly came on my fifth birthday. I had moved on from Teletubbies and developed a new obsession with Pokémon. The plentiful array of evolving creatures captured my heart. I cheered them on in their quests, championed their friendships and joined them in a mutual hatred of Meowth, who tried to foil all their good deeds.

Knowing that my heart was now firmly in the hands of Pikachu and not Po, the adults in my life conspired to throw me a Pokémon party. I wore a peach dress my grandma had made especially for the party. And then the moment came. My mum walked out of the kitchen holding the cake topped with glowing candles and the room erupted into a tuneless rendition of 'Happy Birthday'. She placed the iced Victoria sponge down in front of me and my heart sank. There, at centre stage on the cake beside Pikachu and Charmander, was my – and all the Pokémons' – arch nemesis, Meowth! Children are terrible at hiding their disappointment, and I was no different. The character I had defeated so many times in my battle fantasies was now smiling up at me, made of royal icing. I couldn't believe my parents had got it so wrong!

We all suffer those small (but at the same time earth-shattering) situations as children, and that was mine. I clung to it for a long time – some might even suggest I'm still not completely over it. Weirdly, I've been able to let go of other, far more serious, problems, much more easily. But there was something else I had to get my head around – something that threatened to blight my future happiness.

4

Culture clash

Straddling two cultures comes with some big challenges. I'm British. I was born in Britain and have spent most of my life here. But my first language is Cantonese, and I spent my formative years in China. Therefore, I can find myself torn between these cultures, and I often hear my friends who are mixed-race say the same. Like me, they grew up with different influences, customs and heritage.

My parents have a different approach to family, raising children, work and lifestyle from many British families. Sometimes other people don't understand that. We have to recognise that, just because someone else does something differently, it doesn't necessarily mean they're wrong. We can't impose our own values onto other people's cultures and traditions. In fact, there's space for us all to learn, grow and have new experiences as we live alongside and respect one another.

Juggling these two cultural influences led me to ask myself some tough questions about my identity from an early age. It's hard to work out who you are when you've had such varied experiences and influences. I found myself looking at the people around me and desperately trying to be like them, rather than celebrating the ways we were different. From primary school age, I started to believe the lie that in order to be liked I had to act, look and behave the same way as others whom I perceived to be popular.

There's an additional layer to navigate when you're the child of an immigrant family, as you sometimes start to reject your roots. You can't forget your parents' native language, and you have to eat the food, wear the clothes and remember where you came from. But you also have to fit in where you are, in a place where other kids think your first language sounds funny, they don't like the food you eat and they laugh at your clothes. You have to fit in but not be too Western. You can't detach from your family's values because that means you're pushing back on your own culture, but if you immerse yourself in it too much, you won't be accepted by your peers. Your family is from China, so you *have* to be Chinese. But you live in England, so you *have* to be English. I tore myself apart trying to be just right for everyone. In reality I was being bullied and it was pulling me apart.

In hindsight, I see that the more I tried to find my identity in the acceptance of others, the more I lost myself. Children can be cruel… and sadly, teenagers and adults aren't always much kinder. People are often afraid of things they don't know and don't understand. But I've realised that doesn't mean I have to hide it. I'm better off sharing who I really am.

There came a point where I knew I had to differentiate myself from my parents. I had to recognise that I was more influenced by Western culture than they were. But I'm also really proud to be Chinese. I'm proud of the respect we show our elders and the incredible work ethic my parents have demonstrated. I love the vibrancy of our traditions and want to pass them on to my own children. I want them to eat with chopsticks and to wear red at weddings and banquets as a sign of prosperity. I'm glad I have something different and unique to bring to the table. And I'm sad that bullying led me to reject something so beautiful.

It's taken me a long time, and I've had to unpick all the lies I believed when I was younger, but I am finally finding myself. Sophie. Fully British, fully Chinese – and completely in love with both. My identity isn't tied up in either of these nationalities, but in my character, the way I care for my friends and the things I'm passionate about.

If you're feeling stuck and unsure of who you are, if you're torn between different cultures or demands, that's OK. Many people have been there, myself included. It may sound scary, but taking a look at the things you've allowed to define you (including the opinions of others), and deconstructing the elements that aren't helpful, is a great place to start. Don't let someone else's idea of you or your culture define how you feel about yourself. Don't give more weight to someone else's words than they deserve. Don't let bullies make you believe you're unworthy. It's so easy to carry harsh words around for years, but ridding yourself of them will help you truly understand yourself and who you are. You're beautifully unique. I felt so free as soon as I managed to cut ties with those lies.

Everyone deserves the chance to embrace each and every part of who they are and where they've been. We can all enjoy the rich diversity around us. Share a meal with someone that they won't have tried before, teach your friends a word in another language, speak with pride about the things you've learned from your heritage. These are all pieces of who you are. And you are worth knowing more about.

5
Facing racism

It was against this backdrop of uncertainty about who I was and which culture I truly belonged to that I had my first experience of racism. My school in Darwen was predominantly white. There was a handful of Black kids and one girl from an Indian family, but I was the only person of Chinese heritage. I was seven years old, and my friends and I were thick as thieves in the playground, running around playing tag and seeing who could do a handstand for the longest time. We would pretend we were all sisters and swap shoes or school cardigans, and we all had different coloured glitter gel pens we shared.

Then one day I came into school and everything had changed. Nobody wanted to play with me; in fact, they wouldn't even talk to me, and they all avoided sitting next to me in class and at lunch. Not only did they no longer want to borrow my stuff, but they didn't want me to touch theirs either. The first day, I took it on the chin. Children don't read too much into these things, and I just brushed it off. But it continued, and more children joined in with the shunning as the week went on. Eventually, I went over to one of the girls when she was on her own in the playground and asked why they didn't want to play with me. She told me: 'Because you've got "chinky germs".'

I had no idea what she was talking about. I'd never heard the word before. From the way she said it, I thought I must be ill. I thought I had a bug they could catch, and that everyone should stay away from me. I just didn't understand how I had gone from having friends one day to being totally ignored the next. I sat in the toilet cubicle by myself for the rest of break time and cried. I felt so alone. It wasn't as if it was just one friend, which would have at least allowed me to go and play with someone else – it was everyone. I was completely ostracised.

It was my mum who picked me up that day. I was tearful as I explained that my friends didn't want to touch or play with me because I had 'chinky germs'. Through choked-back tears, I said I wasn't well, and that I shouldn't go to school any more.

That was the day I truly realised what a powerhouse my mum was. She was furious! I didn't know what racism was at the time; I hadn't even heard the word before. All I knew was that there was a problem and Mum was intent on solving it.

When we got home, she immediately phoned the school and asked to speak not just with the head teacher, but with the entire faculty. She marched into that meeting and didn't hold back. She was livid, and made sure the staff knew about it. She explained the damaging effects racism can have on anyone, let alone a child. She made sure they understood that these terms weren't funny and *why* they weren't funny. She impressed upon them why each person should be treated with the dignity they deserve. Mum was well respected as a small business owner in the area and as someone who donated money to the school for safety initiatives and for guest speakers to come in to give assemblies, and they took her seriously. Whenever I think back to that moment, I'm so proud to have her as my mum.

My mum was always tough, and she taught me to be the same. If anyone was ever rude to me, she would tell me to stick up for myself. She was the parent who would tell you to hit the bullies who hit you even harder. She regularly reminded me that no one could tell me I wasn't enough. Mum championed me in everything I tried, and encouraged me to embrace being a strong woman. Having spent so much of my young life away from her, she wanted to make sure that every moment we spent together counted, and she always took the time to share her wisdom with me.

Many of the teachers were horrified at what had happened, and were apologetic. Following the lecture my mum gave them about racial bullying, they gathered the parents to relay the message that prejudicial language had been used and inappropriate behaviour had taken place in the school. Then there was a session with all the students where they were taught about racism.

The feeling among the children was one of shock. Until they were brought in for the session and had the problem spelled out for them, they didn't think they were doing anything wrong. They hadn't realised their words were so damaging. But as a child, you wouldn't. Children aren't born racist, and in most cases they don't want to cause anyone harm. They aren't afraid of cultural differences because they don't see them.

The thing that upsets me most about the situation when I think back on it now is that it wasn't just one careless child being mean. Whichever of my friends started that rumour must have heard the word 'chinky' from a parent; a grown adult, who fully understood how hurtful that would be and how wrong it was to speak about others in that way. I've replayed scenarios where a little girl is sitting around the table telling her parents what she did at school and who she played with, and one of them says: 'Oh, don't play with that Sophie. She's got "chinky germs".' Of course, I'll never know if that's what happened. But I do know that kids don't make this stuff up; they repeat it.

The children apologised to me. And even though I wasn't involved in the conversations, a lot of the other mums went to speak to my mum about it, and I think they said sorry too. A lot of them were embarrassed their children had been a part of something that had caused so much upset. That was when I became acutely aware I was different and *looked* different – and that some people would treat me differently as a result.

In time I started playing with the girls again and we remained friends, but something stuck with me. I still feel sad for that little girl who had closeted herself away in the toilet cubicle, worried she was ill and couldn't have any friends, wondering who she could play with and if she'd be lonely forever. I wish I could go back and give her hug. I wish I could tell her she'd never feel alone again. Sadly, that wouldn't have been true. I didn't know it then, but there would be moments of crushing isolation in my future.

6
Home sweet home

I was eight years old when I finally moved in with my parents. As I was a bit older, I didn't need quite as much attention. My dad converted the room above the shop into a playroom, so Mum could collect me from school and take me there for a few hours while she worked downstairs. I had a few games and toys up there as well as a TV and some of my favourite videos. I would do my homework in the playroom before we went home together for the evening. Given the bullying I had experienced at school, they wanted to keep me closer and make sure they were there to support me if I needed it.

The house we lived in was a modest terrace in the heart of Darwen. It doesn't exist any more, as it was later demolished to make way for a new secondary school, which Shivie would attend years later. On the ground floor we had a living room and a kitchen, and up a flight of steep steps were the two bedrooms – mine and my parents' – plus a small family bathroom. If I was ever in trouble or upset about something I would sit at the top of the stairs and refuse to come down.

The decor wasn't fancy. We had different wallpaper in every room, each more garish than the last. It wasn't like the minimal style you see today; the carpets and curtains all had bold styles with a tea-stained tinge and looked like something from the set of a vintage episode of *Coronation Street*. But although it was nothing grand, it was perfect to me because we were finally together.

I was over the moon to finally be at home with them. I loved spending time with my parents. We didn't argue and I rarely heard a cross word from them. I guess that, because we didn't usually have much time together, they didn't want to spend it telling me off. I had always enjoyed being with them, and from this point on I would be all the time. I was delighted!

When I was with my mum, I felt loved. She made me feel safe. My mum's routines were similar to the ones I had been used to with my grandma in China. Grandma had sung me Chinese lullabies before bed, and a few years later, my mum sang me the very same songs. It immediately felt like home. My mum would read to me at bedtime, and I always asked for *Cinderella*. We would sing 'Ten Green Bottles' round and round in circles, as the first set of ten often fell off the wall before I fell asleep.

Dad started closing the shop on a Monday, so we had a whole family day just the three of us. We would cook together in the kitchen and then sit down around the table to eat whatever we had made. We would always cook Chinese food. My dad, who had a secret obsession with karaoke – just like his mum – would sing songs after dinner. He made everything fun. He worked incredibly hard, but he also knew how to let his hair down. Now that Kelvin, Shivie and I are adults, he's even been known to hit the clubs with us when we go out in China!

We did our best to fly back to see Grandma and Grandpa for Chinese New Year in January or February. There would be celebrations taking place on every corner and decorations everywhere you looked. Dad always made sure we booked a karaoke room and had a few drinks to mark the occasion.

Mum made a point of making sure I had lots of toys. Dad was a bit more frugal, but she always won the battles. She once bought me a toy electric guitar. It had big colourful buttons that lit up and made a noise when you pressed them. I would play with it and dance around the living room, making a racket. When it was clear I loved music (almost as much as my dad did!) she got me one of those echoey toy microphones, and I insisted on staging performances that everyone had to watch.

Not every day was amazing, though. I once came home from school with nits, passed on by one of the other girls in the class. Unable to completely clear them from my thick, long hair, my mum cut me a bob. I was devastated! All I wanted was long glossy hair that I could swing around while I danced and played. To make up for it, she bought me some toy wigs I could mess around with in the house and a Hello Kitty scarf with tassels on the end that I treasured. I would wrap it around my head with the tassels hanging down and pretend it was long hair.

7

Dancing queen

My living situation changed a lot during the first ten years of my life, but there was one thing that stayed the same: my love of dancing. Alongside the singing, and my acting in plays and at school, I loved to dance.

It was my grandma who first introduced me to dancing when I was in China. She didn't enrol me in any fancy classes or teach me the technical names for the steps. She just danced with me. We would stand in the living room, turn up the radio and dance together. I would jump around and do spins and twirls, and she would clap and jig alongside me. She always encouraged me.

Morris, ballet and tap

When I got to England, she told my parents how much I enjoyed dancing. So my mum booked me in for dance classes at the age of four. I know you're probably picturing me as one of those really cool little kids at the front of the dance troupe doing backflips and perfectly executing complex hip-hop choreography, but sadly no one knew about the dance group Diversity back then, and no one knew about those kinds of moves. Unsure of which type of dance I would enjoy most, my parents chose to start me off with morris dancing!

That's right, I was morris dancing at four years old. Mum took me and my two cousins, so we made it a fun group activity. If you don't know what morris dancing is, give it a Google and check it out for yourself. It's an English folk dance that involves rhythmic stepping, performed by a group of people wearing white, and brandishing bells and handkerchiefs. Classes were run at the community church hall. It wasn't fabulous or cool, but it got me started with formal dancing lessons, and I loved it.

It was with the morris-dancing group that I experienced my first dance competition. Sundays were competition days, so we had to wake up at the crack of dawn to get to the church where the bus would pick us up to take us to the contest. I loved competition days because my mum would always stop at the butty shop on the way, where we'd buy either a sausage-and-egg butty or a big breakfast barm. The staff would hand over a white paper bag that instantly became soaked and see-through from the grease seeping out. My mum would get a piping hot coffee in a polystyrene cup and a rubbish lid that wouldn't have protected the liquid from the lightest breeze.

When my parents saw that I wanted to dance as much as possible, they put me in for ballet and tap lessons. I was about seven years old at this point, and it was these classes that really helped me develop my timing, sense of rhythm, and ability to remember and work to choreography. Even so, I didn't enjoy them. I was too young to find the technical aspects of dance interesting, and I often felt bored. I wasn't interested in the strong, slow movements of ballet, and I didn't care about the poise or ladylike expressions. I just wanted to stomp around to loud music! By this point, I was always at an afterschool club of some sort, whether it was dancing, acting, swimming or something else, and all these groups were really fun and open and nurturing, but I didn't get the same feeling from the ballet and tap classes. There was something draining about the atmosphere. The sessions were gruelling, and not at all the uplifting experience a class for children should have been.

Dance school

I walked into my first proper dance school, Sanderson Dance Studios in Blackburn, when I was ten years old. They held the lessons at a venue called Tony's Empress Ballroom. It was an art-deco hall with huge windows and parquet floors; rickety, but with so much character. The place has closed down now, but it was iconic in its day, and dubbed 'the home of northern soul'.

By the age of ten I had worked out the kind of dance I wanted to learn, and this was the closest place to our house that taught street dance to young people. I walked down a grand spiral staircase in this beautiful old building and into my first class. The song we danced to was 'Don't Cha' by the Pussycat Dolls. I felt so grown up, and quickly begged my parents to sign me up for more classes.

This became my Saturday routine. I would spend the whole day rotating around different rooms at Tony's Ballroom, learning various types of dance. I would always start the day with street, followed by cheerleading. Then in the afternoons I tackled ballroom and Latin.

I would also stare through the little windows in the doors of the other classrooms to watch the dancers. That's when I discovered freestyle disco. Once again, I went back to my mum and begged her to let me take up this new genre of dance. In these energetic lessons, they taught me to cartwheel, and to do the splits and elaborate spins.

As freestyle was a solo dance I didn't need a partner, but I knew we would have to pay for solo lessons before I could consider competing. Even then, I would have to be good enough for the dance school to invite me to be a part of their team.

My solo teacher was Lucy. She really took to me, and I looked up to her. She was the strictest teacher, but her students were the best. Lucy saw a lot of potential in me, and encouraged me to keep going with my dancing. Down the line, she persuaded me to audition for dance college.

Competition time

I entered my first solo competition when I was ten years old, having thrown everything I had into my training. I ended up with bruises all down my legs from jumping and landing in the splits. My feet developed blisters and bled from continuously practising tight spins, and I had splinters in my feet from the old wooden floorboards. The day before the main event, I went to get a full-body spray tan – and they didn't hold back. That distinctive orangey-brown hue was a staple on the dancefloor of these competitions, and I couldn't run the risk of appearing too light-skinned.

I was entered for the beginners' freestyle disco round, and I got up at 5:30 a.m. to prepare for the day. I didn't want to leave anything to chance. I started by washing the biscuit-smelling outer layer of spray tan off my body, then crimping my long hair into a voluminous mane. Looking back at the pictures, I slightly resemble Hagrid from Harry Potter, but when it came to getting ready for dance competitions, more really was more! Next came the make-up. I had a glittery eyeshadow that I applied up to my eyebrows, a blusher for my cheeks and a bright-pink lipstick to complete the look. Then I just slipped my pyjamas back on and wore a dressing gown for the drive to the venue: Hyndburn Leisure Centre in Accrington.

My mum took me, and on the way she stopped off at the McDonald's Drive-thru to pick up some breakfast. I ordered a Sausage and Egg McMuffin and a summer fruits-flavoured Oasis. This soon became our routine before any competition, and I always looked forward to that cheeky breakfast treat before what was always a very long day.

We arrived in Accrington at 8:30 a.m. and queued to register at 9 a.m. It was cold outside in the queue, but those who got there late would be given a high number and wouldn't be in the first heat for their dance. So an early number was vital for the competition. Some of the other dancers had worn their school tracksuits to the venue, but I was still in my pyjamas waiting to get in.

When they opened the registration, we signed in and I was given a big number to attach to the front of my costume. I went and changed into my outfit – a plain, second-hand yellow-and-green spandex ensemble. I wore a green leotard and yellow cropped leggings with a matching yellow headband. In the beginners' category you couldn't have too much glitz on your costume. You weren't allowed rhinestones or glitter until you moved into the starters' category, the next level up. That was handy for us because the one-on-one lessons had cost so much that Mum and Dad couldn't afford the kind of elaborate outfits the more experienced girls wore, a lot of which started at £1,000. The dressing rooms were like a chaotic scene from a film, with people flapping about everywhere, preening and applying new layers of fake tan. There was a constant hairspray fog in the air and every surface was taken up with makeup and hair clips.

It was another five hours before I would get to compete. The partners' rock 'n' roll was up first, followed by the presentation of the prizes for that event. Then it was the team dance, and their prizes were dished out. First in the afternoon was the under-12s' freestyle disco. I was up! I took my place on the well-lit dancefloor with a table of judges at one end and onlookers surrounding the rest of the perimeter. There were fifteen or so other dancers on the floor, and we were told to always move anti-clockwise to avoid bashing into one another mid-routine.

It's a strange feeling knowing someone's watching your every move, assessing you and judging you as you dance. I felt petrified, and conscious of every part of my body. I plastered on the biggest smile I could muster and started to move to the music. I shimmied across the lacquered floor in what felt like a rhythmic version of *The Hunger Games*, desperately trying not to put a foot out of place and to survive till the end.

I didn't place in that competition – by which I mean that I wasn't first, second or third. But something clicked in me. I felt invigorated. I loved taking to the stage, and I knew I wanted to do more of it. I also benefited from the discipline needed when a competition is coming up. It taught me to be consistent, and that consistency leads to results. Having the accountability of my teacher and the goal of winning a competition was inspiring for me, and I started to work even harder.

The only thing I struggled with was some of the other girls. Anyone who knows teenage girls knows they can be vicious, but in a competitive environment the effect was magnified. Even at that very first competition I felt a coldness from some of the others, and the 'mean girl' attitude was a common feature in the dance world. As I moved up the ranks from beginner to starter, then to intermediate and eventually champion, the coldness eased a little. I always felt I had to prove myself to fit in, but I didn't really understand the rules of how to do that. If I wasn't picked for something I was treated badly as the others assumed they were better than me. But if I was picked for something I was treated badly because the competition was so fierce they would resent me.

A winning streak

I started placing in my fourth competition, and from then on the trophies, medals and certificates began rolling in. My mum collected every single one and displayed them next to the TV on the living room wall. Freestyle dancing was my favourite and, spurred on by my winning streak, I trained five times a week. As I wasn't naturally flexible, I constantly had to stretch to build up the suppleness required for some of the more gymnastic moves. Lucy would attach weights to my ankles and make me practise high kicks. Then, when she took them off, I would be able to kick far higher as my whole leg felt lighter. It took two years of training at the dance school for them to ask me to join their team for competitions. It felt like a huge achievement, but only meant I had to dedicate myself further to the dancing to make sure I met their high standards.

The biggest event I won was a three-day dance festival in Wales, which involved intensive rounds and tough competition. After the exhausting weekend they handed me a six-foot trophy and put a crown on my head. I still have photos of Lucy and me posing with the giant award, the thick layer of mascara I had applied streaming down my cheeks. The trophy was so big it wouldn't fit in Mum's car, so she had to work out a way to strap it to the roof before we drove home.

She was immensely proud of every win, but she wasn't a pushy 'pageant mom'. The competition days were so long that she would sometimes go and take a nap in the car while she waited until it was my turn to compete! I spent that time hanging out with friends and watching the other rounds of dancers. I was really fortunate that my mum was so supportive, because there was a raft of negative feedback headed my way, both on and off the stage. It would have been impossible to bear without her steadying influence.

A flying visit

Dancing was a big part of my life, but I also joined the Blackburn Cathedral choir. This wasn't just a turn-up-and-screech-with-your-mates-for-a-laugh job; the choirmaster worked hard to make sure we were all singing to our highest potential.

A representative from the cathedral had come to my school, where he heard a number of us singing our hearts out. I was one of the few they selected to join the choir. He handed me a letter to give to my parents, inviting me to come along to a rehearsal at the grand old church. Mum took me along the next weekend, and I loved it. I loved to perform and had always jumped at the chance to be in the school plays. This was a great opportunity to do more of the same, and I ended up singing with the group for years. We performed at all kinds of events and for all sorts of important people.

One of the most exciting experiences for me as an eight-year-old came when the choirmaster announced we would be flying out to Prague for a performance. I was so eager to go and sing in a completely different country! We were there for a couple of days and slept in very basic dorm rooms at a Czech monastery. Not many people can stay they've stayed in one of those!

The performance itself took place in one of the ornate church buildings in the city centre. Only we weren't singing in the main hall; it was a stunning, candle-lit concert in one of the crypts. At least – I might have considered it stunning had I been an adult rather than a child who was terrified to go down into the basement of a creepy old church!

Opportunities to take the stage and sing kept on coming with the choir. My favourite time of year was Christmas. We would be booked up every weekend for carol concerts and festive events. We sang all the old classics you'll remember from school, such as 'Silent Night' and 'Hark! the Herald Angels Sing'. Every performance was accompanied by candles, and that Christmas smell hung in the air.

People were always in such a good mood, and they actually sang along cheerfully rather than just mumbling under their breath, as they did in most other services.

I've always loved Christmas. My parents and I went to Midnight Mass together on Christmas Eve. Even though we didn't really engage with the religious side of the festive season, we embraced the culture of it, and I was always excited at being allowed to stay up so late. After a nervous sleep and a visit from Santa, we'd all bundle into the car and go to my auntie's house in St Helen's for the day. The house was packed full of Christmas decorations, presents and all my cousins running around playing with their new toys. The table was piled high with a buffet of traditional British Christmas food (pigs in blankets, thank you very much) along with a full Chinese feast. It was beautiful carnage.

8

Handling rejection

Around the time I began competing in dance competitions, I also started going to auditions for acting jobs. I became good at handling rejection, partly because I'd had a hard time with bullies at school and partly because any competitive hobby like dancing or acting involves going head-to-head with people who are talented. It means losing and being told 'no'. Even though my dancing was constantly improving, I didn't always win, and I wasn't always selected at auditions either.

Facing rejection in these two, very different, scenarios left me with mixed feelings. On the one hand, rejection could be a positive influence. Someone who wins all the time is rarely a humble person. We all need to know what it means to lose so we also know how to win well. Losing inspired me to improve and helped me appreciate the incredible skills of others around me. It put a fire in my belly and made me want to keep working and growing. But I was always supported in those rejections by my parents and by Lucy. They helped me to pick myself up when they came, and to make a plan to do better next time.

The rejection I faced throughout my school life and even from my friends because of my Chinese heritage was far harder to process. There was no picking myself up and working out what I had done wrong or how I could improve, because I wasn't wrong. I was being targeted for something I had no control over. It made me retreat into myself, and I felt simultaneously exposed and alone. That type of rejection is something no one should have to face.

It made me question whether I was good enough, and it made me feel I had to work extra hard and achieve extraordinary things to prove myself. But that's not right. That feeling of insecurity did spur me on to get better at dancing and to do well in my career, but I could have found that motivation from a place of knowing I was enough rather than feeling I had something to prove.

These days I don't take rejection as a reflection of my worth, and you shouldn't either. I can see now that some things just weren't to be for me, and it's good to let those things go. That doesn't mean rejection is easy to deal with, but I allow myself to feel the disappointment and then I move on.

If you've been rejected in the first way I described – you've put yourself out there in a healthy way and it didn't work out – you need to know that it's OK. Most of us will apply for a job we don't get, attend an interview for a flat share we aren't offered or fancy someone who doesn't fancy us back. That doesn't mean we're not good enough; it just wasn't the right fit. If it's in the context of auditioning or competing, it still may not mean the other person was better. Sometimes it's about timing or how you were feeling that day, or something specific the judges or casting directors were looking for. It's not personal.

If you've been rejected in the second way I described – for your race, gender, religion, sexuality or anything else – it's hard not to take that personally. But from someone who has been there, you need to know that it says more about them than it does about you. No one should be judged based on one characteristic like that, and if someone responds badly to you for one of those reasons, you don't want them in your life anyway. Believe me.

The people you surround yourself with should love every part of you. They should be interested in the things that make you different from them. They should be curious to learn about your experiences and, above all, they should be your best cheerleaders. That doesn't mean they shouldn't call you out if you're being rude or unreasonable, but they should have your best interests at heart in every situation. They should never make you feel as though you're not good enough.

Picking yourself up after a rejection like that can be hard. You may feel vulnerable in new friendships or new relationships, or you may become defensive in an attempt to protect yourself. But know that you are enough, just as you are. You are worthy of love and kindness. Horrible people walking out of your life is something to celebrate, not mourn.

9
The school of hard knocks

I was eleven years old when I started at Queen Elizabeth Grammar School (QEGS). This grand old institution was a forty-five-minute drive away in Blackburn, so I had to get up at 6.30 a.m. to make sure I caught the school bus. If I missed it my mum would be furious, as it meant she had to drive the hour-and-a-half round trip to drop me off.

It was a fee-paying school, which was well beyond our family budget, but my parents were adamant they would make it work. My dad never went to school because his family couldn't afford the bus fare, so he wanted to be certain that I got the best possible education. I was the only person from my primary school to go to QEGS, so I faced the daunting task of making a whole new group of friends.

The school was proud of its rich history. It was initially established in 1509, the first year of King Henry VIII's reign, and moved to its current site in 1884. That's the location I walked into, drowning in my oversized blazer on my first day.

The campus was huge, with various sports facilities and a swimming pool that had to be accessed by coach, as it was over on the other side of the grounds. Each building looked like an old church you might visit on a school trip. Built from old stone, the doorways were arched and some of the windows were ornate, with leaded divides. I sat in the main hall and imagined that I was at Hogwarts. The high vaulted ceiling was held up by a series of wooden beams, and long dining tables lined the room. There were church-pew-style benches alongside each table, and brass chandeliers hung from the ceiling. The teachers wore long robes from their own graduation days at assembly. And if you were unlucky enough to be issued a Saturday detention, you had to attend in your school uniform.

I had been so impressed by the vastness of the school on the open day that I felt sure I wanted to attend. But if I'm honest, the *St Trinian's* film had recently been released, and I imagined having a similar experience at QEGS. Far from forming a sharp and scheming girl gang, however, I ended up surrounded by boys. The school had only recently switched from being a boys' school to co-ed, but it was still nowhere near fifty-fifty. Having grown up in my aunt's house with my wrestling cousins, I wasn't fazed by the idea of being outnumbered.

The problem when your parents scrape together every penny they have to send you to a private school is that most of the other children there have no problem paying their way, and then some. The wealthy pupils all had the latest phones, gadgets and accessories. Having financially crippled themselves just to get me through the door, there was no way my parents would be buying me a Baby-G watch or a flip phone on a contract. During my time at school I was always one step behind my peers. Looking back now, I'm so grateful for the sacrifices my parents made for my education, and I didn't want to put any strain on them by asking for more, but as a teenager, desperate to fit in, I found it tough.

I preferred the creative subjects at school, and always looked forward to art and games. The benefit of going to a posh school was that a range of sports was available to me, so I swam, and I played football and tennis. When I got older I had the opportunity to take ice-skating and snowboarding lessons at the dry slope in nearby Haslingden.

As well as my studies, I was juggling a lot of extra-curricular activities. I had started auditioning for modelling and acting roles in the summer before secondary school started, and was beginning to be offered jobs and roles. While I was still in Year 7, I was cast in a feature film called *Grow Your Own*. I played the daughter in a family of three refugees who were given a plot of land within a Merseyside allotment, an act that ruffled some feathers among the local gardeners. It was a light-hearted British comedy about community and pulling together, featuring Olivia Colman and Benedict Wong (who played my dad).

This would have been a far more exciting experience if it hadn't been for the terrible response I received from the other kids at my school. Rather than seeing it as an interesting addition to school life, the other children felt challenged by this achievement. They didn't like the fact that I would sometimes have to leave school at lunchtime to film, or spend a week or so out of school, learning from home or on set. They taunted me as I left, feeling I wasn't entitled to the special treatment I appeared to be enjoying.

I was given a huge, thick script that I took around with me so I could constantly be learning my lines. Sometimes I would have to take myself away at break or lunchtime to read the next scene we were filming and memorise my part. The other kids often took the mick. Sometimes they hid the script and refused to tell me where it was. I dreaded going back to school after taking time off for filming, partly because I wondered which creative way they would use to make fun of me next, and partly because I started to get more and more behind with classwork, despite my best efforts to keep on top of it.

At home, my parents praised me for my hard work, both in my filming and my studies. They were so proud of all I was achieving. But at school it was a different story. There, I was an outcast, shunned by my classmates. On reflection, it seems obvious that they were jealous. It feels weird for me to say that, but it was clear that some of the children felt there was some sort of competition going on. One girl told everyone she had been scouted directly by Simon Cowell, and that she had also been cast to appear on *Coronation Street*. None of it turned out to be true. I didn't want any part in this competition; I just wanted a quiet life with my friends. Despite all the flak I was getting, I tried to be kind to everyone.

This already uncomfortable situation was exacerbated by my race. Once again, I was in an environment where I was the only person who looked like me. The school was predominantly white, with a handful of students from Indian and Pakistani families. To the children there, the fact that my parents had worked their way up from nothing to develop skills and invest in their own business meant nothing. All they saw was that Sophie's mum and dad owned a chippy, and to them that was hilarious. As with most schools, there was nothing ingenious about the nasty nicknames the bullies assigned to their victims. Sophie Lee became 'Soggy Wee', just because it rhymed.

It was around this time that I started receiving more cutting racial insults. I would be called 'slit eyes' and 'chink', and was told to go back to my own country. Some of the boys went around at breaktimes, sneaking up behind the girls and pulling their skirt down to reveal their underwear. It wasn't just me who fell victim to this horrific prank, but I still remember someone creeping up and yanking at my skirt. It dropped to my ankles in front of a group of lads who laughed hysterically as I desperately tried to pull it back up to cover myself.

I wasn't popular with the boys at school and didn't even consider dating until I was fourteen or so. I wasn't the fit girl, or the one everyone thought was pretty. The girls who got the most attention were the blue-eyed cheerleader types with swooshing blonde hair. And that just wasn't me. I plucked up the courage to ask a tall boy I had always fancied from a distance to our end-of-year prom. His response was: 'Why would I want to go with *you*?' It gives me a lot of satisfaction when some of the boys who were really horrible at school send me messages asking to take me out, which I, of course, ignore.

At times the teachers' responses were also hard to stomach. Competing in dance contests, I often had to put on fake tan. One teacher pulled me up in front of the whole class to ask what was on my skin and to tell me I looked awful. I called my mum in tears, and she stormed into the school to put the teacher straight.

I didn't have the confidence in myself at that time to stand up and be who I was, to own my achievements as well as my mistakes. Instead, I did what most teenagers do: I put up a wall. I was so desperate to be accepted that I started acting up and became the class clown. I was disruptive in lessons and argumentative with the teachers, all in the hope of impressing the people who were treating me so badly.

The more I acted up, the more my grades went down, and I started dropping into the bottom sets for maths and science. The teachers put me 'on report', which meant I had to carry a grey card around for my form tutor and head of year to sign, documenting my behaviour each day. At one point I was even upgraded to a red card, which had to go straight to the head teacher.

Being the 'funny one' gave me a mask. If anything, it meant people made more jokes at my expense, but now it was part of my persona to brush them off and laugh along. I created a character that didn't take anything too seriously, and that way the bullies couldn't see how much I was hurting.

Not everything at QEGS was miserable though, and in time I developed some real friendships and found an element of hope in the teachers who championed me. I have fond memories of singing Rhianna's 'SOS' in a school talent show, and constantly carrying lip gloss and Maybelline's Dream Matte Mousse in my bag. I'll always laugh about the day when there was a problem with the school bus. Mum bundled all the kids from my stop into her car and dropped everyone at the school gate in her dressing gown!

I remember walking around the Royal Armouries Museum in Leeds on a school trip and looking at all the incredible kit people had taken into battle, from a Japanese samurai to Henry VIII himself. I wore my Heelys – trainers that look normal until you flip the wheel out of the sole and skate around on your heels. The teachers were furious when I started rolling around the exhibition and hiding from them.

It was a surreal moment when I was invited back to the same museum to collect a Woman of Honour 2023 award. It felt as if I was coming full circle – only this time I was in heels, not Heelys!

One teacher in particular stands out in my mind for providing just the encouragement I needed. Miss Arkwright was the art teacher, but she also ran the drama club that put on musical theatre shows. She was amazing. I would excitedly show her pictures of me from my dance competitions. When I won trophies, she was full of warmth, praise and support. I felt she believed in me. She picked up on my best traits and encouraged me in them while gently correcting me on the things I was getting wrong. I will never forget the way she saw my potential, even through my class-clown mask. She told me not to give up, and to keep working for the things I believed in and wanted to achieve. I'm thankful that, despite the challenges and loneliness of school, I never doubted that I had her in my corner.

10
My film debut

Lots of the girls from my dance school sent their photos off for modelling jobs, and after a little while my mum started doing the same. She would scour the papers for modelling job adverts and call to see if I could be considered. I started getting booked by Littlewoods and Asda for jobs in the childrenswear sections of their catalogues.

I was ten years old when I signed up with an agency that dealt with both modelling and acting. Having come across some of my catalogue photos, they reached out to Mum to see if I would be interested in auditioning for acting roles. I had adored performing in plays at primary school, and would later enjoy being part of productions at secondary school. When Mum finally agreed to put me forward, it felt as though every performance, living-room play and Avril Lavigne talent show performance was finally paying off.

I was taken on by an agency called Kids International, which met up with me and Mum and took a load of headshots to send around to casting agents. Not long after they sent off my pictures, they called to say I'd been offered a modelling job. I couldn't believe it – I didn't even have to go to an audition! The job was an advert for Vimto. For those of you who haven't tried Vimto, you are really missing out. It's a sweet, fizzy liquid with a flavour that is hard to pin down. It's a combination of fruit and spices, but I would say it has a unique unique taste.

We had an early morning call-time for the shoot, and I had to go to a grand old mansion in Manchester with a swimming pool in the back garden. I wore a bathing suit and lay on a bright purple inflatable dinghy, bobbing along on the water. They told me to pretend I was floating in a pool of my favourite fizzy drink (which, for the purposes of this shoot, was obviously Vimto). They gave me a massive bendy straw and I spent the day taking fake sips, making yummy noises and pulling funny faces for the camera. The pictures were used on posters and billboards. Once we were driving to dance school when a massive purple lorry drove past us with my face plastered on the side. The excitement of that moment was immense. I felt like I might bubble over like a shaken-up bottle of Vimto.

I got a few other smaller jobs, which were a lot of fun, but when my agent called to say I had an audition booked for a film, that's when I got really excited. We weren't told who was in the cast, or even the name of the movie. None of that had been confirmed when I first heard about it. The agency told us the film was a heart-warming story with themes including immigration, community and the way different cultures interact. I would be auditioning for the role of the daughter in a refugee family who had moved to the UK from China.

The young girl I would be playing in the film was called Phoenix. I loved this name and the imagery it evoked. The picture of a pile of ashes suddenly morphing into a stunning and majestic bird had always appealed to me. It felt poetic and powerful. I was convinced this was the part for me.

Sadly, it's not always that simple. Actors convince themselves that each part they audition for is the one for them, but the casting directors often disagree. You never know what they're looking for, so rather than try to work it out and give them what I thought they wanted, I decided just to be me.

Ahead of the audition, we received an intimidatingly large script in the post. I stared at it, wondering how on earth I would remember a whole film's worth of lines. A small part of me thought it would actually be a relief if I didn't have to. It was the first movie script I'd ever seen, and I was struck by how co-ordinated it all was. Details about the camera positions, and the mood and tone of the delivery, were all meticulously laid out. The closest thing I could liken it to was when my dance instructor gave directions about the tiniest details of my form or facial expression – because she knew how she wanted the moves to look, and they had to be perfect. This was when I found out that film production was the same. The director had a vision, and it was the actors' job to dance to his tune.

The production team considered several young girls for the part, but I didn't cross paths with any of the other hopefuls. They kept all the actors who were in direct competition away from each other. I went down to London several times to read for different senior members of the crew: various producers to begin with, and then, as I got further through the process, the director Richard Laxton. When I made it to the final round of auditions, they explained that I was up against one other girl. My character in the film would have a younger brother called Dragon, and they had already cast a young boy called Jeffrey Li in that role. I found out on the day of the final read-through that I was up against Jeffrey's biological sister for the part. I felt sure I wouldn't make it, knowing they had the option to run with a real-life set of siblings.

My mum got a call shortly after the audition to say that the director really liked me and I had got the part. I was beside myself! I was convinced I wouldn't be able to sleep a wink until the day we started filming *Grow Your Own*. Every night I went to bed with the excitement of a kid on Christmas Eve after leaving the mince pies out for Santa.

The production team had been impressed by the high level at which I spoke both English and Chinese. Apparently, that's what clinched it for me. We did have problems with my speech when we started filming, however, because they wanted this Darwen-bred girl to speak broken English with the accent of someone who was new to the country and had grown up in China. It took me ages to get a passable lilt to my voice, but eventually they were happy that I didn't sound like a lifelong northerner.

Mum and I stayed in the Holiday Inn in Liverpool most of the time so we were close to the Merseyside set. The production company had rented a plot of land set back from the seaside and created a whole allotment for us to film in. The schedule was gruelling, and I often had a 6 a.m. call-time. I would start the day in hair and makeup. Mine was obviously minimal, as I was playing a schoolgirl, but my hairstyle was always a ponytail or two bunches, which I loved. After the glam squad had worked their magic, I would be driven to set for 8 a.m. Often, it was still dark as I pulled up. There's a lot of waiting around on any set. The camera operators may need to reset, or there may be a problem with the sound or they may want to wait until the clouds move over so they can get the lighting just right.

I would amuse myself by messing around and playing little pranks. I would whisper jokes into the microphone so only the sound team could hear. Sometimes when we were filming a group scene, I would do my best to pull a silly face and hope no one would notice so they would leave it in the edit. One of the faux gardens in the allotment was 'growing' some very real, very delicious, strawberries, and I got told off for munching on the set a couple of times.

I was too young at the time to realise just what a big deal some of the other actors were. Among them was Olivia Colman, although she wasn't to rise to the meteoric levels of Oscar-winning fame for many years. The film was set out as a series of smaller stories experienced by the residents, all of which converged on the allotment. Olivia's scenes were mostly shot when I wasn't on set, as our narratives didn't overlap much until a big scene everyone was in together at the end. I remember saying good morning to her in passing on the few occasions we were filming on the same day. She always had a big smile and a cheery, upbeat tone.

Omid Djalili and Eddie Marsan were also in the film. But as a young girl I didn't have the confidence to strike up a conversation with the adults, especially the professionals! I kept myself to myself, supported by my mum, and mainly spoke when I was spoken to.

The actor I did spend a lot of time with was Benedict Wong, or Benny as he encouraged us to call him. These days he's busy playing Doctor Strange in the Avengers franchise, but in *Grow Your Own* he was my dad. His character was mute and suffered from PTSD following a traumatic journey to seek refuge in the UK. Our fictional family had arrived in Britain after stowing away in a shipping container, and my mum had tragically died in transit. As Benny's character did not speak, and I was the elder of the two siblings, my character did most of the talking. I spoke in a mix of Cantonese and the best broken-English I could muster for the film.

When he wasn't playing the deeply troubled on-screen character, Benny was a lot of fun. Having grown up in Manchester, there was some overlap in our social circles, and he already knew a few members of my extended family. He hung out with us and played around, making jokes and winding me up when he thought I fancied one of the young lads in the film. I remember that his Chinese wasn't great, so we would mess about and I would correct him on some of his pronunciation.

I was totally in awe of his acting. When we started rolling, Benny transformed into his character in an instant. I learned a lot about professionalism on set from him. Seeing him being perfectly happy to mess around at lunchtimes but then hearing him say, 'Come on now, guys. Let's focus and be professional. Let's get it done,' once we were on set was a great example for me as a young girl.

After all that hard work, there were two parties to attend. First, the wrap party once the final scenes had been shot. This was held at a bar in Liverpool on our final day of filming. I was in the last recorded scene, and there was a tangible sense of relief when the director shouted 'Cut!' and then 'That's a wrap!' Recording for a film is gruelling and the director was meticulous. Often the same scene would be shot over and over again to make sure we had all the angles and options needed for the edit. After all that hard work, everyone was ready to let their hair down. I only stayed for the first hour or so, as it was late, and I was far too young to head out on the town with the rest of the cast.

Second, and far more exciting, was the premiere, which was also hosted in Liverpool. It was on a school night, but Mum let me attend. I remember my English teacher setting some last-minute homework that day to be turned in the following day. I explained that I wouldn't be able to complete it, as I would be at my movie premiere, and she was less than impressed. I appreciate the importance of schoolwork now in a way that I didn't when I was actually studying, but that moment was a once-in-a-lifetime experience for me. I definitely don't think sacrificing it for an English comprehension quiz would have been the right decision.

We stayed at a hotel near Liverpool's city centre, and I got all dressed up for my first glitzy event. I walked down the red carpet, which was lined with press. Of course, they wanted to talk to the big-name stars rather than me, but I didn't care; I felt like a star either way. I'd seen red carpets on TV a million times, and now I was actually walking down one. It was a proud moment for my mum too, who had taken the time to accompany me to every rehearsal and filming day. Attending the final glam party and watching the film all the way through was probably just as special for her as it was for me.

For my mum, a woman raised in a difficult household with hardly any money, who had moved to the UK in search of a better life and opportunities, the overall message of the film really hit home. The way we welcome those from other countries and cultures has been a huge theme in her life, and in mine too. While my mum had possessed a plane ticket and was legally allowed to move to the UK, her family had still risked a great deal to get their new start on British soil.

The film still pops up on TV from time to time, especially around Christmas. Whenever it does, I get messages on Instagram and WhatsApp from friends telling me it's on. I think back over that experience really fondly. At times I wondered if it would be the biggest achievement of my career. In my darkest days, I thought I never wanted to be on camera again. But I had no idea what my future held.

11

Smells like teen spirit

I was a slow starter with boys and dating. They didn't seem interested in me, and I wasn't interested in them. I didn't have my first kiss until I was fourteen, which was a lot later than many of my friends.

Outside of school, my time was filled with dance classes, competitions and events. I met one of my oldest friends, Briony, on the dance scene. She was part of a team from Burnley, and I would watch her dance at shows with amazement. She moved so naturally; she wasn't self-conscious, but just flowed with the music. I admired her talent. I was thirteen when we first met, and I approached her at a competition and asked if I could have a photo with her. I really looked up to her.

When we kept bumping into each other, we got talking and just clicked. No one was ever mean to Briony. She was tall and slim like a Barbie doll. I felt protected when I was with her because she was fiery and popular. She didn't let anyone say a bad word about me. I loved that I had a friend who stuck up for me. Up until then, it had felt as if I was alone against the bullies when I wasn't with my mum.

She moved to my dance school when I was fifteen, and we became inseparable. We would go to class together and hang out afterwards. For some types of dance the advanced competitors were paired up with a partner with the same level of skill. I was with a boy called Sam, who, after a few months, decided he wanted to stop dancing altogether (something I said?)! With a lack of boys around, I was paired up with Briony. At first it felt weird to be dancing partner dances with another girl, but then we realised we were the lucky ones. We each got to rehearse and dance with our best friend.

The two of us went to parties together. At sixteen, we got fake

IDs and took them out on the town in Burnley. We were obsessed with whether or not we could pass for eighteen, and tested each other on our fake dates of birth, names, star signs and anything else bouncers could ask to catch us out. I was never massively into alcohol. My friends were interested in getting their hands on booze for their nights out, but that didn't excite me too much. When I did drink, it was the fun, fruity drinks I was interested in, like apple schnapps or blue WKDs. No one in our group of friends used drugs, so they didn't factor in my life.

I did what most teenagers do with their parents and insisted I wasn't hanging out at parties with boys, and that I wasn't drinking. My mum was no fool, though; she definitely knew more than she let on. What mattered to her was that I was safe, so if I went out, she insisted on dropping me off and collecting me at an agreed time. Sometimes Briony's mum would do the drop-off and mine would do the pick-up, or vice versa.

Moving to Blackpool

Once my school years were over, I decided I wanted to go to dance college. My instructor Lucy encouraged this ambition. Dance had become such a big part of my life that I knew I wanted to continue to take it seriously, and maybe even make a career out of it. I pushed myself to be the best; to prove to my parents that I was worthy of all they had invested in me and all the sacrifices they had made. In a move that was very reminiscent of a teen dance movie, I even missed my final German GCSE exam so I could attend college on the day of the auditions.

I found out I had secured my place after a letter dropped through my door with what I hoped was an offer. I couldn't bring myself to open it, so I scooped it up and took it to my dance class to show Lucy. I flapped it around in her face, and she had to snatch it off me to read the words on the page. I was excited to go to college and learn more, but I was also excited to make her proud. She had always believed in me and had encouraged me to keep going and aim for the next big achievement. This was as big as they came at that time.

In order to attend, I had to move to Blackpool for three days a week. I stayed in a shared house specially designed for dance students at the school, and hosted by a couple who were former pupils.

College opened up many new opportunities, challenged me to perfect my technique and pushed me to improve. But most of all, it humbled me. I had gone from being one of the best at my local dance school to being surrounded by people who were training for the most difficult competitions. I was no longer the best; I still had a long way to go. My training had mainly focused on gymnastics and flexibility, and these were great skills to have on my side, but I also needed to develop the strength and discipline of the classical training I had missed out on when I stopped my ballet and tap classes.

What I wasn't prepared for when I started was that I would be one of the youngest there. The majority of students had completed their A levels and started college at the age of eighteen, but I had come straight from my GCSEs and was only sixteen. I felt displaced, especially being away from home. My peers would go out clubbing and drinking, and I couldn't join them because of my age. Once again, I was the only Asian girl at a primarily white school. I was also aware that, while I was by no means overweight, I was larger than some of the other, very petite, girls. For the first time I started to feel self-conscious about my weight.

My first boyfriend

I was seventeen when I got my first boyfriend. I was in my first year of college when out of the blue I got a message on Facebook from a guy called Theo. I was already aware of him, as we had loads of mutual friends. He was involved in gymnastics and parkour (where you find the most creative and athletic way to get from point A to point B – watch *Casino Royale* if you need a visual example). He was two years older than me and good-looking. He lived in Preston, halfway between Darwen, where I lived, and Blackpool, where I stayed when I was at college. I was flattered by his attention, especially as I knew he was popular, and we started messaging online every day. After a couple of weeks, he suggested we meet up. It was July, but not one of those normal disappointing Julys where it rains constantly, and we all complain that we haven't seen a glimmer of sunlight. That year, July was blazing.

He suggested I come to Preston and said he would pick me up from the station. I didn't tell my parents I was meeting a boy, as I knew all hell would break loose if I did. Instead, I said I was going into college and then got off the train early in Preston. Before I got there, I had scoured the internet for as much information about him as I could find, and came across a very active Tumblr account. This is now a defunct social media platform just for pictures, basically a prehistoric Instagram.

When I saw him walking up the ramp towards the train platform, my first thought was, *Thank goodness he looks just like his pictures on Tumblr!*

Theo was tall and had an athletic build, although he wasn't muscular. He had highlights in his hair, which he kept up in a quiff, like Justin Bieber circa 2013. He was tanned with freckles, and had the kind of eyelashes that women swoon over but men don't notice. His arms were covered in tattoos of snakes and roses. I didn't know if they had any personal significance to him, but I liked them. He wore a snapback cap, jeans and Vans trainers. He walked up and smiled at me, looking like the centrefold in every copy of *J17* magazine ever made.

The date was a typical teenage hangout. He picked me up from the station and we drove in his dinky Fiat 500 to Avenham Park in Preston. We sat on a bench and chatted. I felt self-conscious that my fake tan might start sweating off in the heat. My hair was curled and I wore denim shorts, a white T-shirt and red Vans. I had my iPad in my school bag, and we joked around, taking silly pictures of each other. I liked him, but we didn't kiss. It took another four dates before I felt comfortable enough to kiss him. I wasn't experienced with boys, and had only kissed a couple in the past, so I wanted to take my time.

We ended up dating, on and off, for five years. The first couple were turbulent. We would argue over little things and then spend days not speaking to each other before making up. There was a lot to like about Theo. As well as being very good-looking, we also had a real laugh together, and we shared many moments of kindness and gentleness.

I also adored his parents. They lived in a house right out of town, surrounded by fields and farmland. Their home was like a haven of peace. He would drive us out there, and we wound around the small country lanes, singing songs together the whole way. The playlist featured anything from Neo to Linkin Park. We went there on Sundays before I headed on to college in Blackpool for the week. If the weather was nice, we'd mess around in the garden. I taught him how to do the splits and challenged him to handstand races. He loved to draw and write poetry, and we drank unlimited cups of tea as we whiled away the afternoons.

Sadly, the arguments steadily got worse, and two years or so into our relationship, we started actually 'breaking up' after each one. These break-ups sometimes lasted days or even hours, but once it was for six months. He had bought me a chunky chain necklace with a sweet link clasp at the front for my nineteenth birthday, and every time we split I took it off. It was a far more accurate indicator of our relationship status than looking on Facebook.

For a while, Theo worked at a club called MACs in Preston. I would go there from time to time, and after chatting to the manager I was offered a job. They wanted me to be one of the glam girls who walked around selling shots to revellers out on the dance floor. Theo was fuming. He hated the idea of me invading his Saturday nights, and didn't want me chatting to other men while I was working. I took the job anyway, and he eventually adjusted to the idea.

A major bust-up

Once I had completed my three years of college and received my diploma, I was excited to get out there and start dancing for a living. Unfortunately, Theo didn't approve of my chosen profession. He had known since we met that I wanted to be a dancer, but now the time had come for me to audition for jobs, he was completely against it. He didn't want people looking at me, or for me to get any attention. He never wanted me to wear the makeup and glam outfits that were often part and parcel of the job.

For one job I was performing at the Miss Swimsuit UK competition in Leeds for two days. He called at midnight on the first day and demanded I come home immediately. He told me if I stayed, he would have a panic attack. I felt that he wanted to keep me locked away; that he was worried he would be left behind if my career took me to amazing places. That was his own insecurity speaking.

Theo certainly had mental-health struggles, and sometimes he would throw them at me during an argument. If we fell out, he would tell me I had made him want to hurt himself. As a young woman, I didn't know how to process that. In a rational sense, I felt I wasn't responsible for his low moods. But I couldn't help feeling I was to blame.

There's no doubt in my mind now that the relationship was toxic. Theo was toxic, but so was I. I often wanted my own way, and was upset when I didn't get it. I didn't have a clue what healthy communication looked like at that age. It's easy for me to list the things he did wrong, but I know he would also have a list of instances when I behaved badly.

After a while, Theo's aspirations changed. He launched a YouTube channel and started body building, so we couldn't eat out any more. He had to be so careful with his diet that he couldn't order from a normal restaurant menu. He didn't want to go out for drinks or to a club either, because he didn't like me being looked at by other men. So we spent the last year or so of our relationship sitting on the sofa together every evening.

I started to feel low, like I was missing out on life. Life with my friends, dancing, having drinks and being silly at weekends. Life with a boyfriend I could have fun with, and who wanted to go on adventures with me. And life with a career that didn't fill me with dread because I knew every success would lead to an argument.

We finally called it a day after five years of dating. I had planned a fun double date for me and Theo, along with his brother Jordan and a friend of mine. When the night came around, Jordan didn't show up, leaving my friend feeling embarrassed and disappointed. I was furious, so I texted to tell him off for being so cruel and careless. I got an unremorseful response. He said he'd rather go on a night out with me instead, and that I was dating the wrong brother. I was completely taken aback. I went straight to Theo and told him about the conversation, but it sparked days of arguments about why I had been messaging his brother in the first place. It was the start of the end.

We had a huge bust-up, and Jordan took Theo to Thailand for a lads' trip to get him over our break-up. He came back after a couple of weeks and dropped me a message, asking if we could meet up. Very quickly we were an item again, but a couple of months later he sat me down to tell me he needed to go and 'find himself' in Thailand. I suspected he had met another girl on holiday with his brother, but he never confirmed whether that was the case. He packed his bags again and flew out to spend a few months working and discovering himself.

12
The greatest grandparents

It was while I was at college and dating Theo that my grandma passed away. I was nineteen years old at the time. The loss of any family member is heartbreaking, but losing my grandma felt more like losing a mother. I was at home for the day and the phone rang in the early afternoon. It was my dad's brother ringing from China, and he wanted to speak to my dad. When Dad got off the phone, he told Mum what had happened. Then Mum came up to my room to speak to me. I felt as though my heart had torn in such a way that it would never be mended.

Grandma was in her eighties, and she had lived a good life. Even though I didn't see her as regularly during my primary and teenage years as I had during my first five years, she had still often come over to the UK for long stretches, and we had made the annual trip to China. I felt bonded to her, and suddenly that connection was ruptured. I would never be able to laugh with her, cook with her or dance around with her again.

My mum's voice broke as she slowly told me what had happened. There had been a flood in their village, so she had ridden on the back of one of her neighbours' motorbikes to help with the water damage. When she was finished, she had headed home and laid her head down for a short nap before dinner. But she never woke up.

It warms my heart to know that she was comfortable when she passed, asleep in her own bed. It's the best way for anyone to move on from this life, and she deserved the very best.

I was too young to know how to process that level of grief, so I simply ignored it. My initial response was one of shock. The world went silent, like someone had hit the mute button. I cried at first, but then I felt numb. I was supposed to go and work the tills at a clothes shop in the town centre, and I still went. I couldn't bear the idea of sitting around in intense pain with my family.

My dad flew out for the funeral, but he was the only one of us to make the trip. It's unconventional for a young, unmarried person to attend a funeral in our culture, so I stayed at home and tried to honour her and say goodbye from a distance.

I still miss her every day. I laugh when I think about her permed hair and the gold tooth she got because it was the most cost-effective option. She never cared what people thought of her. Women with her confidence, care, kindness and character are few and far between. I have always aspired to follow her lead.

We were all worried about Grandpa. All he'd known was life with Grandma, and now she was gone. He was still surrounded by family, as he lived with my dad's eldest brother and his wife. In Chinese culture, we don't have care homes. There's no question that elderly family members must be cared for by the younger generations. Even so, Grandpa struggled to adjust to life without his soulmate. For the last five years of his life, he had to endure the heartbreak of being without her.

He passed away in 2019, just months before the global pandemic of 2020 kicked in. I'm pleased he didn't have to live through that difficult time. Hearing the news of his passing, again from my mum, was bittersweet. I thought back to every moment of flying kites together and the inventive ways he had mended things for me. I thought of how he had taught me to say 'please' and 'thank you', and the way he had always scooped me up onto his lap. I felt desperately sad that he was gone. But I also knew that he was with the love of his life, my grandma, once again. I will never stop being grateful for what they taught me and for the amazing gift they were to me.

13
A trip to Thailand

It was around this time that I moved to Manchester to base myself in the big city and embrace all the opportunities that came with it. We were both living in a new setting and looking for a fresh start. The problem was, Theo kept calling me. He would call when he'd had a few drinks, sometimes asking to borrow money, and sometimes just wanting a chat. I couldn't stop myself from following him on social media. I would see him in restaurants or out on day trips and imagine the women lurking just out of the frame. None of this was healthy, but neither of us was any good at completely cutting the cord.

After a few confusing conversations, he assured me that he wanted to come back from Thailand and move to Manchester with me. I decided I needed closure. Either we needed to be together properly or to split up for good.

Having just been paid from my job at a flashy Manchester bar called Menagerie on the Sunday, I went straight online and bought a ticket to Thailand. The following day I was on a flight to surprise him, and to find out what he actually wanted for our future. I took a care package with me containing his favourite biscuits, a box of Yorkshire Tea, some tops and a cap.

I knew he worked at a tattoo parlour in Phuket, so I got a taxi directly to his work. My heart raced when the cab pulled up outside. I took a deep breath and walked through the parlour door, exhausted from the thirteen-hour flight, my suitcase trailing behind me.

I immediately made eye contact with Theo, but it took him a moment to register who I was. It was so unexpected that he couldn't quite compute what he was seeing. After a couple of seconds his brain caught up with his eyes, and his face dropped. He hustled over to me, asking me in a low voice what on earth I was doing there. He didn't seem pleased or relieved to see me; he was panicked and furious.

We had a rushed conversation. He told me he couldn't talk because he was at work, but he would call me later. I went off and booked myself into a cheap hotel. I had spent all my money on the flight, so luxury was out of the question. It was directly opposite a 7/11, so I grabbed something small to eat, then sat in my room and cried my eyes out.

I stayed in Thailand for a week. Theo spent that time avoiding me and ignoring my calls. I remember sitting on the beach in a daze, watching the water lick the sand and retreat again. I had cried so much that I didn't have anything left to give. The sense of isolation and heartbreak felt insurmountable. I took out a pen and paper and wrote it all down: every upset, frustration, confusing conversation and argument, but also all the good times, the inside jokes, and the moments of kindness and care. I wrote that I was grateful for what I had learned. Then I went to the tattoo shop and handed it to one of his colleagues to pass on.

Theo finally messaged, and we arranged to meet up for a drink to have a conversation. I spent hours getting ready for our big showdown. I wanted to be sure that no hair or bit of makeup was out of place.

The conversation was cold. He told me he'd been seeing a young Korean woman he had met in Thailand. It was clear that neither of us thought there was anything left to salvage. I felt hurt, broken and betrayed.

I flew back to Manchester and took some time to close the chapter. I threw myself into my work and hung out with my closest friends. I didn't rush back into dating, but paced myself. My decision to fly out to Thailand may sound spontaneous and a bit like a young, silly girl in love… and that's exactly what it was. My head was scrambled, and I needed answers. It was a brutal way to get them, but at least I knew for sure after that.

While he was in Thailand, Theo was accepted onto the Thai version of *America's Next Top Model* called *The Face*. He didn't win, but he enjoyed the attention the show brought with it. He later

1 I loved to play dress-up! Here I am (aged 2)
   in a dress handmade by my grandma.

2 (Left to right): Mum, Grandma, me (aged 3) and Dad flying
   back to England for the first time after living in China.

3 Competing in my first ever Morris-dancing competition (aged 4).

4 Competing in another Morris-dancing competition (aged 4).

5 Dad wearing his best hat at my fifth birthday party.

6 My first freestyle disco competition in my
yellow-and-green spandex ensemble.

7 Heading off to high school in my new uniform (aged 11).

8 I loved wearing wigs and fancy dress when messing around and performing at home (aged 11).

9 Competing in a freestyle disco competition (aged 15).

10 Putting my flexibility to the test at dance and gymnastics training (aged 16).

11 Sometimes a dancer, sometimes a mermaid! Working in the Manchester nightlife scene (aged 21).

12 One of my first fire-dancing gigs (aged 21).

© Amir Shah

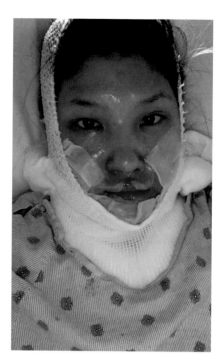

13 Me in hospital in Chicago just after the accident (aged 22).

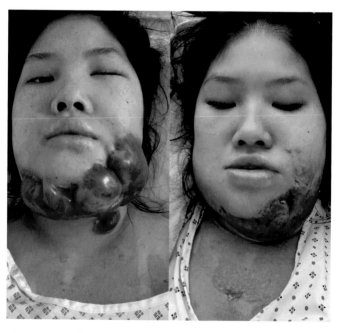

14 After leaving hospital, my scars quickly grew into keloid tumours.

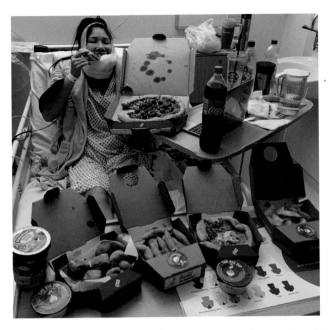

15 Back in hospital to have my keloid scars operated on and my friend
bought me a massive Domino's delivery. We had a pizza party!

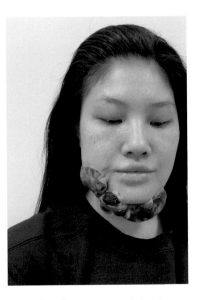

16 After the cryogenic injections,
the scar tissue started to die and
turn black. It eventually fell off.

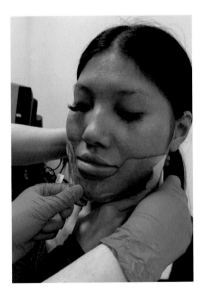

17 Having my compression
mask fitted.

18 Happy to be heading into schools to talk to pupils about my journey and what it's taught me (aged 27).

19 Honoured to have won Influencer of the Year at the 2023 Beauty Awards.

20 I now do a lot of public speaking to share my experiences with others.

moved back to Manchester with his Korean girlfriend, who became his wife and later his ex-wife.

Moving on from my first boyfriend of five years wasn't easy at all. I thought it would be the hardest thing I would ever have to go through, but I didn't realise then that worse was yet to come.

14
Knowing your worth

Knowing your worth doesn't always come easily. Even now, I have to regularly remind myself that I am valuable, and worthy of love and care. I forget those things in the way we all do. But sometimes it's not that we've forgotten; it's that we never knew it in the first place. It was a long road for me to build myself up after being badly treated at school and in my relationship with Theo. It was easy for me to think I deserved it all, because I didn't really know any better.

When it comes to dating, we can all let our guard and our standards slip, especially when we really fancy someone. In that exciting honeymoon phase, it's easy to allow small things to slide, even if we wouldn't usually settle for them. We can feel validated by having someone's attention and having a fun, flirty conversation going with them. But sometimes we all need to take a step back and ask ourselves: Is it OK that I'm having to wait so long for replies? Or: Is it OK that he can be a bit mean and then say it's just a joke?

I find it helpful to ask myself: What would I want for my best friend? We're always so much kinder to our friends than we are to ourselves. We fiercely protect them and build them up. When they're not sure of their worth, we remind them. Sometimes it's easier for me to take a step back and work out if I'm where I want to be or if I've just been blinded by my feelings.

When I'm struggling with my self-worth and don't feel great about myself, I often think the worst thing I could do is date. I've gone through long stints where I didn't date at all because I needed to focus on myself. Being unhappy and lacking confidence isn't a good foundation for a healthy relationship. You're far more likely to choose the wrong person or settle for less than you're worth when you're in that place. Using dating as a tool to validate or feel better about yourself is more likely to leave you feeling worse than when you started.

When I don't feel good about myself, and my self-worth is low, I remind myself of how far I've come. I'm a totally different person from the one who dated Theo and was so excited to have the attention of the fit lad everyone fancied. I now know that a guy liking me (or not liking me) doesn't affect my value at all, but I didn't know that back then. We can be so focused on the grind, on what we don't have and haven't learned yet, that we forget to look back and praise ourselves for our progress.

I'm proud of my achievements and of the strength I've shown in difficult situations. I know that if I was able to get through those dark days, I can definitely get through the one I'm going through. Just like you, there is only one me. Only one person who will live my life, one person who has my character and quirks and passions. That makes me infinitely valuable. I'm irreplaceable. And so are you.

15
Fire in my belly

It was 2017 when I truly settled down into Manchester life and tried to move on from Theo, the turbulence I had experienced in Thailand and the eventual break-up. I had loads of different jobs at this time in my life. At one point I even joined a girl band called Limited Edition. There were five of us, but we never got a record deal, and differences of opinion meant the whole thing fizzled out.

I worked in various bars and took 'shot girl' jobs in clubs, while I continued to audition for dancing roles. It wasn't long before I started being hired to dance at events and for club nights. I would wear glitzy outfits and be up on the podium, leading the dance floor with my energetic moves. I liked the nocturnal life. I would often work in a bar until midnight, then go and dance at a club until 4 a.m., then move on to an after-hours club to dance until 6 a.m. It was exhausting, but I felt I was at the centre of the action. If I wasn't sleeping during the daytime, I worked as a promo girl and model for different brands. I could be modelling at a trade fair one day and outside a university handing out Greggs vouchers the next.

I kept trying to get my foot in the door with full-time dance positions and regularly bought a £5 coach ticket from Manchester to London to audition for P&O and Disney cruises. I didn't get those jobs, so I carried on working the nightlife scene in Manchester until I came across a few people who incorporated fire into their performances. They danced, but the real money came from the fire-breathing. I was intrigued by the idea of it. I'd seen the performers in clubs before and on TV, but had assumed it took years to learn how to do the dangerous moves. I never considered it as a potential career.

They invited me to rehearsals and said they would teach me the basics so I could give it a go. The first time I held the fire, I was terrified. I could feel the heat coming off it and warming my face. I felt unsteady just holding it out in front of me, let alone swinging it around and running the flames along my body.

The first thing I learned was the safety aspect. You can never take too many precautions when you're working with fire. I had to learn how to work with the paraffin and exactly how much I needed to keep my sticks alight. I was warned never to wear hairspray, always to keep my hair tied back away from my face, and not to put any cream or moisturiser on my skin on the day of a show. I was also told to keep a wet flannel and sand bucket by the stage when I was performing.

Then they showed me how to perform. The moves were no problem. I was a trained dancer and gymnast, so the routines were fun and easy for me. But it was a whole different ball game when we added in the fire. If someone told you to walk along a ledge that was a foot off the ground, you could do it no problem. But if someone told you to walk along that same ledge at the top of a skyscraper, your legs would start to buckle, and you would feel as if you might fall off at any minute. The action is the same, but the stakes are higher. That's what the fire performing was: high-stakes dancing.

My first hurdle was to get comfortable with the flames. I started by swinging the sticks around with gentle movements, adjusting to how they felt in my hands. I got used to the distance they needed to be from my body and how the fire created a trail that followed behind as it swung. I watched YouTube videos of fire performers to see how they moved, and the character they created when they were dancing with the flames. I felt empowered. When I was dancing around, commanding the blaze, it made me feel in control. I was fierce and sexy and dangerous, and that's the character I adopted. Theo and I weren't together by this time, but I knew he wouldn't have been happy about me performing in this way.

The first move I perfected was running the fire up and down my arms and legs. That was simple enough to do without scalding myself, as long as I kept up the pace and didn't actually touch my skin. Much like walking on hot coals, it isn't painful providing it's over quickly enough. Then I learned how to put the flames out with my mouth. While it looks as if fire performers are extinguishing it on their tongues, in actual fact they let out a deep, sharp breath as they lower the fire towards their open mouths, which puts it out without making any contact with the mouth. I practised this and perfected the skill, feeling like a magician performing a trick by sleight of hand.

Finally, I learned how to breathe fire. For every performer, this is the most eye-catching spectacle of the show. It's done by taking a mouthful of paraffin and holding it there until you're ready for the grand finale. Then you blast it out of your mouth and onto the fire to launch a spectacular flame into the air. It's not a safe thing to do, but you can make it as safe as possible with careful positioning and control. All of this takes thorough instruction, precision and practice.

Once I had mastered each of these moves, I wanted to take to the stage to try them out. I didn't feel ready to perform, but no one ever really does. Like a stand-up comedian, you've just got to get yourself onto the stage and see how it goes. I approached Karina, the boss of a bar called Menagerie, and asked if I could perform there. Karina always encouraged and called out the best in me.

True to form, she wanted to give me that chance. She told me to come in during the day to do an audition for her and some of the team. There were other performers and dancers who would be auditioning at the same time. I watched them move to the music so cleanly and classically. The acrobats contorted their bodies in unbelievable ways and the dancers never missed a beat. I suddenly wished I was just there to dance; I knew I could have done that. But what I was doing was different from what everyone else was doing, and it was a completely different type of show for me.

My turn came around, and I stood before the small audience. The music started and I lit the fire batons. And then I froze. I suddenly forgot every bit of sassy, fierce energy and felt as if I were glued to the spot. I moved around a little, but I was stiff and uncomfortable. There was no performance; I just couldn't get into character. I totally flopped, and then I felt so disappointed with myself.

Before Karina could come across to give me the bad news, I walked straight over to her and said, 'That wasn't me. It wasn't my best. Give me another chance to show you what I can do. Let me come back again tomorrow.'

I turned up the next day with the same equipment, but this time I had a new perspective. I wasn't going to mess this up. I was going to show Karina how I could move and command the attention of the room. I changed my song to a Beyoncé track, and right then she was the only woman I wanted to duet with.

I got up on stage, and this time I wasn't focused on being sexy. I wasn't trying to move my hips to make people lust after me. I wanted to show everyone I was powerful. I wanted them to see that I could hold danger in the palm of my hand. I wanted to embody female empowerment.

I brought the house down. The difference in performances was like night and day. Karina immediately agreed that I could perform one night a week.

That one night a week quickly increased to two and then three. Soon, other venues were getting in touch to ask if I could perform for them, too. I started to become known on the Manchester scene as the girl who breathed fire. I met another performer called Chemise, and we started taking joint bookings and performing together. She was good to me, and I looked up to her. I admired her drive and boss mentality, but most of all I admired the fact that she wanted the women around her to succeed. Our network quickly grew, and we created a team of talented artists who would come and set parties alight all over the city. I felt alive. I was at my strongest when I was on stage.

16

Never the same again

I started receiving corporate bookings, and these paid far more than a regular slot at a club. Big galas, award ceremonies and fundraising events often wanted eye-catching acts to wow their high-profile guests.

Sometimes this involved international travel. On 1 April 2018 I was invited to perform at a trustee event for a big organisation in Chicago. I got there a few days beforehand, and on this occasion my parents joined me for the trip. We set ourselves up in the hotel the company had booked for my stay.

On the day of the show, we joked about it being April Fool's Day. This didn't feel ideal for me performing, but I'm not superstitious, so I thought it was funny rather than cautionary. That year it also happened to be Easter Sunday and, annoyingly, Theo's birthday. We hadn't spoken for a while by then, so I pushed it, and him, to the back of my mind. I decided not to message him the first birthday he would be spending without me.

By this point my fire dancing had earned me some attention on Instagram, so I left the hotel that morning and headed to down-town Chicago to take some photos for my social media and to look around the shops. I was nervous about the performance that afternoon, but I also felt good. It was one of those days that was cold and crisp but the sun was still shining, and it warmed my face as I walked.

I went to the venue just after lunch, well before the event started. Safety is paramount when it comes to performing with fire, and as this was a new venue I had to start all the checks from scratch. I set out my equipment and made sure it was all in order. I had my fire sticks on one side and my fire fans on the other. These were five sticks attached at the base, so they could fan out and provide five flames in one. I poured a metal cup of paraffin ready for the fire-breathing finale.

I made sure the safety sand bucket and damp towel were by the side of the stage. I checked that the aircon and any other ventilation systems would be turned off during the show, and that there was nothing flammable on or near the performance area. The stage was up against a wall in the middle of the room, with circular banqueting tables beautifully laid out around it. I checked everything twice and three times, and felt satisfied that it was all as it should be. If I allowed myself, I would sometimes got into my own head a bit before a big performance, so the systematic and clear routine of getting set up became meditative to me.

Next, I had to get myself ready. I enjoyed getting into my costume and applying the makeup. I felt as though I was transforming from everyday Soph into my fiery on-stage character. For this show I was wearing a stunning red leotard covered in sequins and gems with a halter neck, teamed with a pair of heels. You can't cover yourself in accessories for fire-dancing, because hats, gloves and loose clothes all pose a safety risk, so the outfits were usually reasonably minimal.

I was in the dressing room when all the guests arrived and took their seats for the dinner. There was an introductory speech from one of the bigwigs in charge of the event, and then they all tucked into their food. There were a few performers who came on later in the evening, and I was to appear directly after a singer. When he went on, one of the event organisers came and got me. I waited on one side of the stage for him to finish so I could get out there. I couldn't tell you what he sung; I was always in the zone before a performance. I had tunnel vision, focusing on my routine and what I had to do, so everything else melted away into a blur of background noise.

I checked that all my equipment was in place one final time, and then it was my turn to take the stage.

There was a bright spotlight pointed at me. I could hardly see the audience; just the outline of people sitting in chairs around me. The stage was set away from the diners, so I wasn't worried about them getting caught in the flames. Despite having done this a thousand times, I felt more nervous than ever for this particular performance. It just felt different somehow. It was a big event, and I wanted to impress. I wanted to be the act they remembered and talked about on the drive home.

I stood at centre stage and put on my widest cheerleaderesque smile. Then the music started. I was only performing to one song: 'Crying in the Club' by Camila Cabello. The three-and-a-half-minute performance had been carefully thought through and choreographed. I started slowly as the song built up, rolling the batons along my arms and legs. Then I switched to using the fan and twirled it around my head in time with the music. Next, I put out a couple of flames with my mouth, careful to disguise my out-breath so the audience would be none the wiser.

Then came the grand finale. I danced to one side of the stage, where I took a swig of the waiting paraffin, then continued to move with the music as I positioned myself with my head facing away from the audience. The music swelled, and I waited for the final line before the big finishing chorus Camila sings about warming your body by embracing the heat from a thousand fires. I let the lyrics linger for a split second and then, just as the beat dropped in a roaring crescendo, I blasted the liquid out of my mouth and directly into the flame. The sound of it cracked over the music and I heard an audible intake of breath from the audience.

This is always the biggest moment of the performance; the part most people could never picture themselves doing. It looks majestic as the imposing flame fills the air above in a plume of heat that radiates through the room.

Through all of my training, I'd been told how important it was that I didn't look. We're working with fire, not playing with it. Opening your eyes for any length of time with naked flames so close could damage them. As I prepared myself to peek out, I knew something felt different. For a millisecond, I peered through my lashes. I expected to see a jet of flames ahead of me, but I didn't.

The fire was coming straight towards my face. The heat instantly engulfed me.

I had no time to react, but it also felt like the longest moment of my life. I gasped and fought to breathe while the flames grew, suffocating me. Some of the paraffin had dripped onto my cheek, chin and chest, and the fire clung to it like magnets drawn to metal. The agony of knowing something was seriously wrong but being on stage, part of a show, a spectacle, felt crippling. If I hadn't been under a spotlight I would have screamed, flapped and rolled around on the floor. Instead, I kept my back to the audience and desperately tried to pat out the flames without causing any alarm. For the first few seconds no one realised anything was wrong. It took a moment for the rest of the room to catch on that this was not in the script.

I started to smell my skin cooking and my hair burning under the heat. I could feel it creeping up my face. I was worried for my eyes. I had my wet flannel to the side of the stage, but going over to get it would waste valuable seconds and could cost me my eyesight.

My adrenaline had kicked in, and suddenly I was in survival mode. I kept hitting my chest and face to put out the flames. The audience realised I was on fire and in pain, but they looked on, paralysed, eyes locked on the horror that was unfolding and unsure what to do. I heard gasps, but I was so intent on extinguishing the flames that I couldn't think about it. I was on fire for less than thirty seconds in total, but that was all it took to change my life forever.

One of the event organisers came over to take my arm and escort me off the stage. I staggered next to her, wondering why no one had brought any water over. They took me backstage and placed ice wrapped in a towel around my chest and neck. It turned out this was the worst thing they could have done, as it resulted in an ice burn on the already fragile skin. What I needed was water, but no one knew that at the time.

I couldn't get my thoughts together. I felt lightheaded, and when I think back to the sounds around me, all I remember hearing now was white noise. A member of staff had dialled 911, and the emergency responders sent paramedics, the fire brigade, a police car and a group from the military. It was surreal. In my haze of shock, I couldn't work out who all these people were or why they were there.

They swarmed around me, and I was lifted onto a trolley so they could get me into the ambulance. They pushed me out through the staff entrance of the venue to the emergency vehicle at the back. I was scared, and my whole body felt cold. My face was starting to swell, and I could feel it tightening up, as if a fist was wrapped around my neck. My oesophagus started to close, my chest was tight. I was gasping, trying to explain to the people around me that I couldn't breathe. I needed air. It felt as though I was drowning. There was all this fuss around me, but I couldn't hear it. They injected me with some strong painkillers, and the faint sound of sirens provided the soundtrack for the journey.

I don't know how long it took for us to get to the hospital, but I do know that the moment we arrived, medical staff were waiting to rush me to the burns unit. I stayed on the trolley, surrounded by people running to get me into a bay in the emergency room to start treatment. I felt overwhelmed by the urgency and started crying. I was so tired. I wanted to close my eyes, but every time I did so, a nurse said in a firm voice that I had to stay awake; that I should not fall asleep under any circumstances.

The tightness continued to take over my neck and the lower half of my face. I reached a hand up to touch it, to see if I could find a way to release the pressure, but it felt huge. My neck had swollen into bulbous pustules that took over my neck and face. I pulled my hand back, trying to work out what I had just touched. When you get burnt, your body sends water to surround the affected area and cool it down. I didn't know that at the time. I just felt terrified. The stench of burnt hair and skin still lingered all around me, despite the pungent smell of cleaning products and chemicals found in every hospital.

When they got me into the right bay, one of the nurses dressed me in a blue gown and another put a hair net over my head. As she adjusted my position to put on the hair covering, some bits of my hair and skin fell onto the bed. I looked down and saw me, my own skin, falling away from my body. That's when I realised how serious the situation was. This wasn't going to be a quick fix. I had done some very real damage to myself.

The medical staff covered me in yellow gauze sheets dipped in an oily substance to keep my skin from drying out and cracking. Several doctors came into the partitioned area while I was there, and the first pulled the curtain all the way around so we had complete privacy. There were people everywhere, working away like ants in a highly productive colony, every single person knowing their job and efficiently getting on with it. All I could hear was rustling: the rustling of stiff uniforms, the rustling of papers as people noted things down, and the rustling of sterile packets being opened.

I was still struggling to process anything. People spoke to me, but I don't remember what they said. My neck had swollen so much it was as if someone was pressing a balloon filled with boiling water up against my skin. The doctors kept coming in and then going away again. They were monitoring my body and how it was reacting to the burn in order to decide on the best course of treatment. A burn isn't like a broken leg, where you pop it back into place and then let it heal. You need to wait to see how the skin reacts to the injury before you can decide how to fix it. I drowsily tried to acknowledge the doctors when they came in. My eyes opened and closed as I drifted in and out of lucidity.

And then nothing.

They finally allowed me to fall asleep.

17
Hospital

I was in John H. Stroger Jr. Hospital of Cook County, a medical centre that specialises in caring for the military and has a long history of cutting-edge burns treatment. That was why the military attended the scene of the incident, as I was to receive treatment from their doctors. I later found out that the fire brigade has to attend any accident involving fire, and that the police were called as a precaution in case there had been any criminal activity or foul play. I didn't think about any of that at the time, though. I didn't think about anything.

It felt as though someone had weighed my head down. My face was so swollen that I could only open my puffy eyelids enough to get partial vision. I had a tube coming out of my nose to help me breathe, and there was no way I could talk. My throat and neck were strapped up and agonisingly painful.

My parents were standing by my bedside when I fully woke up. They had been there for a couple of days, but due to the heavy medication I had been drifting in and out of consciousness without even noticing they were there.

Once I was sufficiently awake to understand and process new information, a nurse came over and explained what had happened over the past few days. She spoke to me about the medication I was on and how they planned to proceed. I slowly tried to tell her that I needed to fly home, but it came out in muffled whispers. She told me I was nowhere near well enough to fly, and that I would need to stay with them until I had recovered. I felt gutted. When you're unwell, all you want is your creature comforts. I wanted my own bed, with my own sheets. I wanted to be near my friends and to have a proper cup of tea and biscuits. I realised I would have to stay in that hospital, miles away from home, and they weren't even able to tell me how long I would be there.

That's when the next devastating blow hit. My parents had to leave. They had pulled in endless favours from friends and family to keep the business open, but they had to go back now that I was awake. I felt desperate and alone. I wanted to beg them to stay; to tell them I needed them and was terrified to be left on my own. But in my stubbornness, all I did was tell them I wanted to be by myself anyway. I felt so hurt that I completely shut down. In the weeks that followed, numerous friends and family members offered to fly out and I rejected every single one. I didn't want to face the pain of them leaving again.

I had one visitor, a friend of my cousin Danielle's. Adam came by a few times while I was in the hospital. Each time, he brought me a care package containing lots of treats, CDs to listen to, and books about faith and Christianity. I hadn't thought much about religion and wasn't sure what I believed. But with everything that had happened, I was open to hearing about a God who loved me and wanted the best for me. In one of the packs he brought a pot of apple sauce. I questioned it, thinking it was an odd gift when there was no spit roast and crusty rolls in sight. He explained that Americans just eat it out of the pot, like a yoghurt or a chocolate pudding. I thought he was winding me up, but after confirming with the nurses, I discovered this was true.

The nurses showed me a lot of kindness, but they couldn't tell me when I would be able to fly home because they had no idea how my burns were going to heal. They didn't know if they would need to operate on me or if I would need a skin graft. I had no idea how the scar would look or whether my face would ever look the way it had before. There was a visible line through the scar on my chest where my halter strap had been, protecting that strip of skin from the worst of the flames.

After a few days I started to get my strength back and walked around my little room. I opened the cupboard to find they had hung what was left of my red costume in there. They had cut it off me, and the top was blackened from the flames. The once-dazzling crystals and adornments were completely charred. I felt disgusted just looking at it.

It was around this time that I started receiving messages from people. Conscious that I should already have been home, my friends started messaging to see why they hadn't heard from me. I wanted the people I loved to know what had happened, but I dreaded telling them.

The first person I called to tell the whole story to was Briony, my best friend and teenage dance partner. She broke down in tears as I relayed how I had been burnt, and announced she'd be over on the next flight. I told her not to come. The same happened when I called my friend Amir. He wanted to jump on a plane straight away, but I stopped him too. By this point I just wanted to be on my own. I was embarrassed by the idea of other people seeing me. I was embarrassed to admit that something had gone wrong at work, in the job that had looked so fabulous and everyone had praised me for. I felt exhausted by their questions because I didn't have answers, as much as I desperately wanted them myself. I wanted to heal a little more before I let the world in. I needed to come to terms with what had happened before I shared it, even with those closest to me.

There was a set routine in the hospital. First thing in the morning the doctor would come round to see me. He would give me an update on my treatment and how my skin was reacting. They wanted to avoid a skin graft if possible, but if they had to do it, it wouldn't be straight away as the skin was too raw and sensitive.

Once the doctor left in the mornings, I had breakfast and the nurses would bring me strong painkillers. My diet was calorie-rich and full of protein, so my body would have everything it needed to rebuild the cells. It was all liquid to begin with, but even this was a challenge because my lips had swollen and they started to peel. They were dry and chapped, so talking, eating and breathing through my mouth became a burden.

After I managed to get my painkillers down, the nurses would take me for a shower. They used a sponge like a scouring pad to scrub at my wounds in order to keep the dead skin at bay and give it a chance to regenerate. It was agonising because they were rubbing at raw skin. It wasn't so painful in the middle of the burn, because the nerve endings there had been cooked. It was around the sides that I couldn't stand the pressure. I would sob as they buffed my tender skin.

I wanted them to stop, but they couldn't. As much as it hurt, they knew it was the best thing for me. I dreaded those morning showers, and I bet the nurses did too. It is hard to inflict pain on another person, even if it is ultimately for their own good. They were kind to me, and I knew I needed their care, but I had never been so aware of my own fragility. I had lain in the hospital bed, dipping in and out of consciousness, and endured various treatments, but it was standing there, naked in the shower, with nurses either side of me and having to endure incredible pain, that I truly felt small. I was exposed. Vulnerable. Broken. And completely at their mercy.

When I got out of the shower they cleaned the wounds again with alcohol, another excruciating daily task to endure. Then they would apply cream and lay gauze on top of the area before dressing the wounds with huge bandages.

The first time I underwent this ritual will be remembered forever as the lowest point of my life. As they wheeled me back to my bed, I caught sight of myself in the mirror. It was the first time I'd seen my face without the bandages. I was red and swollen, and bleeding from all the scrubbing. My hair was messy and singed, and piled up on top of my head. I didn't feel like me. I didn't even feel like a real person. I just felt sick.

In that moment I lost all hope of ever going back to dancing or modelling. I lost all excitement about going out with my girlfriends or getting dressed up for a bottomless brunch. I lost all belief I'd had in meeting a man who would love and care for me, and want to be with me. I couldn't imagine anyone wanting to date me now. I was a freak. Disfigured. I looked like a monster. My life was over.

I screamed and cried, and told the nurses I never wanted to go near another mirror.

After that, my mental health became about as fragile as my physical health. As the days rolled on, I started to feel increasingly hopeless. I felt I was no good to the world. Having other people run around after me, bringing me things and washing me, made me feel utterly useless. I wasn't used to being ill. The last time I had stayed in hospital overnight was when I was born. I considered myself to be young, energetic, fit and full of life, but I felt as if all of that had been taken away from me. If it hadn't been for the nurses, I never would have got out of bed.

Mary is one of the nurses I remember best. She would come over and insist that I get up and have a little walk around. She told me about my circulation, and said that it wouldn't help my wounds if I just laid on my back in bed all day. She would help me get out of bed and slowly walk with me as I did a lap around the nurses' station and then back to my room. If she was going to Target or Walmart on her way home, she'd poke her head in to see if I wanted anything for the next day. Sometimes she brought me little treats even if I'd said no.

I had to stay in a room away from the other patients, as I was at such high risk of infection. Going outside was out of the question, and I couldn't just wander around the hospital. Twice Briony sent me a bouquet of flowers, but both times they were turned away for fear that they would bring bacteria into the room with them.

I was in hospital for a month before I was finally discharged. My mum flew back to collect me and bring me home. Seeing her walk into the ward made my heart feel as though it could float away. The relief of having the comfort of home, of my mum, was so immense that I broke down in tears. I felt like I'd fought through those horrific four weeks to get to this moment, and it was just too much to cope with. I had missed her so much.

I had got used to my little room and, as much as I hated the agonising treatment routine, I felt safe with the nurses who had cared for me. I knew the outside world wouldn't be so kind. Mary gave me a big hug, although she was careful not to press on my burns, and told me I should be pleased to be going home, not worried. I had asked Mum to bring some British trinkets over for me to give to my carers. I had a special gift for one doctor, who always joked that he didn't like Brits. It was a mug with the Queen's face on it. I told him I hoped he would drink a cup of tea from it and remember me – the only British person he actually liked! I gave little keyrings to each of the nurses as a small thank you for their kindness.

I wasn't just fortunate to have those amazing professionals around me, but I was also blessed not to have to pay for my treatment. Without a national health service, a month-long hospital stay in America would have cost more than our family home. But I was able to access the support of a charity scheme for tourists who were seriously injured while abroad in the US. The hospital made the arrangements, and all I had to do was focus on getting better. For this I will be forever grateful.

I left the hospital with my chin bandaged up and my chest completely dressed under my clothes. We had a hotel reservation for that night, and were booked to fly to Manchester via JFK Airport in New York the next morning.

I asked Mum if we could drop by a Sephora store in Chicago before we went to the hotel, as I wanted to pick up some new makeup. I had been told to throw away all my old makeup, as it would be full of bacteria, but I wanted something I could put on the top half of my face, which wasn't affected by the burns. I wanted to try to feel pretty again.

I went straight over to the Anastasia Beverly Hills counter to look at their brow kits. As I was picking out the right colour to match my hair, a girl came over, stared at me and asked: 'What happened to your face?'

I suddenly felt like I was under the spotlight all over again. It dawned on me that I was no longer shrouded in the safety blanket of the hospital.

These days if I sense someone looking at me, I brush it off. I know people are curious. They want to know more about my experiences and how I got my scars. Sometimes it's nosiness and sometimes they want to learn. But back then, I wanted the ground to swallow me up. I didn't want to be different. I didn't want to feel people's eyes burning into me, posing silent questions I wasn't ready to answer. I went cold, put back the makeup palette I had been holding, and went off to find Mum.

I walked over to her and said, 'We have to leave. I can't be here any more.'

18
Big questions

A month alone in hospital gives you time to ask yourself a lot of questions. I replayed the day of the accident and wondered if I had done something wrong or if I'd let something from my safety checklist slip. I saw myself verifying that the ventilation and aircon were off, and arranging my things to the side of the stage. I just couldn't work out what had happened. I knew I had done everything right, and even confirmed twice and three times that it was all as it should have been.

I wondered if a junior member of staff had turned the aircon on without realising how dangerous that would be for me. I wondered if they had all been told not to in their team briefing, or if it had slipped the manager's mind. I would never know for sure. Working with an open flame was always going to be risky, but I never thought I could be involved in an accident like this. I never considered that I could end up in hospital and be left disfigured.

I wondered if I should ever have started with the fire-breathing at all. Should I have stuck to the dancing? Limited myself to what I knew? I was the one who decided to train as a fire dancer; it had been my decision and no one else's. I knew I needed to take accountability for that. But somehow, I still didn't regret it. I wasn't sure if that was my stubbornness, refusing to admit that I had made a mistake, or because, despite it all, I had been where I was supposed to be.

I felt embarrassed, as if I'd let myself down. I had been humbled in a public and visible way. I had to cope with the physical pain and healing, but also a sense of upset that I tried to blank out. I shut people down when they tried to support me, and closed in on myself and my little hospital bubble.

I started to pick back through my life and everything that had been important to me up until that point. I began to feel that I was actually quite selfish and self-absorbed. After breaking up with Theo, all I'd done was focus on my career. I had wanted to audition for bigger and better jobs, and dance on main stages. Ambition in itself isn't bad, but my ambition had only been for myself and what *I* wanted. Nothing on my list of goals was to benefit others, or even to make me a better person for the benefit of others.

I wrestled with myself, my brain telling me I had been a good person and that there was nothing wrong with focusing on yourself. But in my heart I knew that I could have died that day, and I felt sad that I hadn't invested more in those around me – especially those who hadn't had the same opportunities. I wanted to leave a legacy behind that I could be proud of. A legacy my grandma would have been proud of.

While I was in the hospital, the in-house chaplain came to see me in my room. I told him I wasn't religious but had thought about God. He didn't try to push God and the Bible on me; he just encouraged me to live in the light. He said there was light within all of us, and we all get to decide how bright we want to shine. He told me that the moment I decided to live fully in the light would be the most freeing and best day of my life. I've gone back to those words a lot. They were the encouragement I needed at a time when I felt lost.

I've pondered on faith and spirituality more since the accident. I've wondered about the timing, with my life having changed on Easter Sunday – the day Jesus came back from the dead and entered into new life. Maybe that was also the start of my new life… and maybe it wasn't a coincidence.

During that time, I developed a sense of independence that I hadn't experienced previously. I grew an inner strength like none I'd ever known, and the resilience to withstand so much more than I had ever thought I could. I was on the path to becoming a better woman, and that is something else I will always be grateful for.

19
What happened in Vegas...

I was petrified about coming home from the US. I was a different person now. I had been so focused on perfection previously, and now all my imperfections were on display. I still didn't know how my scar would end up looking, but I was prepared for the idea of discolouration, scratches and raised skin. I'd had to let go of the concept of 'perfect' and just feel grateful I was alive. But would others treat me with the same openness and kindness I was trying to show myself?

I might have been out of hospital, but both my body and mind were still unwell. I had a lot of recovering to do, and I felt I had missed out on a month of living by being trapped in a hospital room, unable to go outside and just doing laps of the ward for daily exercise. I think I was still in shock from the whole thing and hadn't processed it at all. I know this, because only a few days after I got back, I made a decision that seemed wild to most people – me included now. I went on a girls' trip to Vegas and LA.

The holiday had been booked for months, way before my Chicago trip. I had assumed I would come back, work for a month, then head off on the fun trip with my friends. When the hospital told me I was being discharged, I realised I would still be in time to join the trip, so I made the bold decision to go. I had already paid for the flights and accommodation, and didn't want to give up any more of my life to this nasty accident. I told my doctors I was planning to go, and they were less than impressed. They warned me not to go out in the sun at all, and to continue with my treatment and recovery. I had to wear a T-shirt by the pool and a cap to protect my face.

I had a pharmacy's worth of ointments, creams and medication that I needed to take or apply daily, so I tipped the lot into my suitcase. I went to see my friend Jay, who also happens to be my favourite hair stylist, and he coloured and cut my hair so it would feel fresh and new for the trip.

I flew out with a group of girls, including Ellie, one of my best friends, whom I had met at a rave in Leeds. We instantly bonded because we were the only ones there in sequined mini skirts and heels! I shared a room with her, and every morning without fail she would start the day by checking I had all the creams and sun cream I needed. She made sure I had fresh bandages whenever I needed them, and that I was always wearing a hat. It was as if I'd taken my mum on the trip with me, but I was grateful for her care.

After being cooped up in the hospital for so long, it felt liberating to go anywhere, and do anything, I wanted. While it may not have been the wisest decision to travel so soon after such a traumatic event, I embraced the freedom. I know now that I was still in shock and grappling with the beginnings of post-traumatic stress disorder (PTSD), as my mood was very up and down.

One day I was sitting in the Encore Beach Club in Vegas, watching all of these beautiful women – many of them influencers – dancing around, jumping in the pool and lying in the sun. From my shady spot under the protection of the cabana, I burst into tears. I wanted to be as carefree as them, but I had to protect myself and cover my chest and face. I felt so ugly. Another friend, Alicia, took me to one side and gave me the mother of all pep talks. She told me I was incredible for even considering venturing out, that I was brave and beautiful, and I should never forget it. She said it didn't matter that I had factor 100 smothered over me or that I couldn't get in the pool. I wasn't letting what had happened stop me from getting out there, and that was remarkable. I felt so encouraged by her words and grateful for the reminder of how far I had already come.

Speaking out

While I was away, I decided to record a video of myself removing my makeup so people could see the scar – the red patch covering my chin and chest – as it really was. Having posted so many glam shots on my Instagram, this felt like a new level of vulnerable. But I knew it was important. It felt like the first step towards becoming the version of me I'd decided I wanted to be in hospital. The version who would speak out for others and represent the under-represented. I hoped this would inspire people who were struggling with their confidence, and even, in some instances, people who had suffered a traumatic physical change themselves.

I wanted to stand up for those who didn't fit in with society's beauty ideals. I wanted people to see that I was owning my scars and proud of what I had learned about myself as a result of them. I wanted to start telling my story, and this felt like the right way to do that. I wanted to show that, above all, I was grateful to be alive. I filmed the short clip and uploaded it, just as it was, with no sound or effects.

I was terrified about seeing the reaction. The internet can be a nasty place. But all I got back was kindness. People said I was unique, beautiful and brave.

This was the first time I had spoken out, and I knew I had to do more.

20
Leaving a scar

I felt a new sense of positivity after that trip. I knew that the road ahead of me would be hard, but I also knew that I could continue to live my life and have fun with my friends.

Then, a couple of weeks after coming home, the scar started to change. The colour deepened and it began to raise up in lumps. It grew bigger than the patches of skin that had been burnt, and extended over my whole chin and neck.

I went to Wythenshawe Hospital in the hope that there would be an easy fix, and the doctors would know how to treat it, but they were stumped. Unsure of how to diagnose me, they said it was probably a hypertrophic scar – a thick, raised scar that isn't responding as expected to the healing process. This can occur in burns victims and, while it's frustrating and doesn't look great, it isn't anything to be alarmed about. They organised for me to be fitted with a compression mask. This was a thick plastic guard that sat over my neck, chin and cheek to put pressure on the scar and reduce its size.

I was in a lot of pain. My scar throbbed, and the mask was difficult and uncomfortable to wear. I was given diazepam (better known by one of its trade names, Valium) to help ease the pain and help me sleep. It did its job so well that I once slept for two days straight. I was constantly drowsy, and missed out on a lot during the months that followed. To my mind it was worth it, as the only time I wasn't in pain was when I was asleep. I felt low, wondering what my life would look like on the other side of this… if I ever got to the other side of this. Sometimes I wondered if it would be better if I didn't wake up at all.

After a while, the doctors still weren't seeing any progress and, as the scar continued to grow, the compression mask became agonising to wear. By this point the scar was taking up so much of my neck that I couldn't turn my head. I had to move my whole body to see anything to the left or right. The doctors had to go back to the drawing board, and they sent me to see a consultant plastic surgeon called Charlotte Defty.

Charlotte took photos of the scar and asked about my pain levels. I talked her through the agony and the difficulty with breathing. I told her it felt as if the scar had a life of its own, and I could feel it pulsing at times. She asked to see me two weeks later to monitor how it had changed. By then it had grown even bigger. I couldn't open my mouth properly and my speech was limited. It was bulbous, and looked bright red and raw. It was like something out of a horror movie.

On seeing it for the second time, Charlotte escalated my case to urgent and told me she was sure I had a keloid tumour. This type of tumour is benign, so I didn't need to worry about cancer, but as keloid scars don't naturally improve, I was terrified I would always look the way I did then. She reassured me they would find answers and come up with a solution.

I was offered intralesional cryosurgery, a new treatment where they inject liquid nitrogen directly into the tumour to freeze it off. This kills the cells inside the skin, and they told me that over the course of the next month to six weeks the skin cells would die, the tumour would go black, and one day it would just fall off. I would be a case study for them, as it was a new procedure and they hadn't used it on such a prominent facial tumour before.

In the run-up to the surgery, I couldn't help but panic about what lay ahead. I didn't want to think about a general anaesthetic, a relatively new surgical procedure and another hospital stay. With everything else I had been through, it felt like too much to handle. My mood was up and down once again. The strain of the situation meant that my mum and I stopped communicating well. It drove a wedge between us. I was pushing her away and she was getting frustrated.

I was referred to a counsellor to discuss how I was feeling and everything that had happened. She was gentle and kind, but I struggled to fully open up to her. I had been offered the standard six sessions under the NHS, and I didn't see the point in baring my soul to someone who would be part of my life for such a short amount of time. So I tried to find another solution for my anxiety.

21
Life of the party

I felt I had missed out on so much that I became frantic. Frantic to make up for lost time. Frantic to prove that I was still fun, and was still living my life to the fullest. Frantic to show that I could do it all: heal, recover and party all at the same time. Everyone copes with challenges differently, and when I was no longer isolating, I launched myself back out onto the nightlife scene I'd been so accustomed to previously. I thought that was the strong and empowered thing to do, but I see now that it came from a place of insecurity.

What I really needed was to be still. I never sat down and acknowledged how I was feeling, or considered the best ways to healthily process it. I just kept trying to live life at 100 miles per hour. I now know that I was anxious and depressed. The tumour was still growing on my face, and I was terrified about the operation. I still hadn't properly spoken to anyone about the accident the year before, and was struggling with the effects of PTSD.

I became reckless in my pursuit of distraction. I did anything I could to get out of the house, surrounded by people and music, rather than being alone with my thoughts. People thought I was a fun party girl. More than that; they thought I was brave for refusing to lock myself away. But in reality, the only thing scarier than being out in public was being at home on my own, left to face reality. On the outside I was happy-go-lucky, but all the spontaneity and laughs were a mask to hide the demons that were eating me up inside.

I was drinking heavily each night out, and on some occasions I got so drunk that friends had to help get me home. I wasn't dating at the time and was completely celibate. I'm grateful that I never ended up burying my feelings in meaningless sexual encounters.

My short-term partying solution was exactly that: short-term. But I would still wake up feeling awful, both physically and mentally. The hangovers took their toll, and after the buzz and party of the night before, waking up alone with a throbbing head felt torturous.

I felt as if I had disgraced myself and my family. I even wondered if I deserved to live. I knew the types of role models I had needed when I was younger, and I was so far away from being that kind of person now. I knew I was being careless, just trying to forget myself. But each time I came out of that party bubble and the light of morning streamed in, I fell back to reality harder and harder. I didn't want to explain myself to the people who cared about me, so I pushed them away.

Down the line, I had to make a conscious decision to stop living that way. I was miserable, and sick of feeling sick. In time, I learned to love myself again, and by extension started to love my own company. I slowly learned to enjoy the peace of solitude, and found I was able to be far more present in the moment when I slowed down. I made the most of opportunities and was able to remember the fun times I had spent with my friends in the morning.

These days I rarely drink. I'll have a cocktail or two on a night out, but my priority is to enjoy time with my friends. I no longer feel the need to be out all the time or constantly busy. It takes a secure person to stop and rest in their own company. I've learned that it takes great courage to stay still in a world that insists we should never slow down.

22

Loneliness

I recently read somewhere that loneliness is as bad for your health as smoking fifteen cigarettes a day. I've experienced periods of loneliness: when I was at school and shunned by my friends; when I was in the hospital away from my loved ones; and even at times when I've been working, surrounded by people, busy and seemingly popular. The reality is, you can still be lonely in a crowded room.

When I was younger, I thought I was lonely because I was unpopular, and that therefore it must be my fault. I deserved the feeling of isolation because I hadn't got people to like me enough to want to spend time with me. But telling myself that meant I pulled away from people more. I protected myself by keeping my distance, which meant I felt even lonelier, and the cycle continued.

There were times when I was hardly ever alone, when I was out partying with a gaggle of people till the early hours. I packed my time with socialising and busyness. But when I looked around me, I realised I still felt lonely. Later down the line, I found that being surrounded by people wasn't what stopped me from feeling lonely. It was being surrounded by the right people. I learned that, rather than investing in the people who were there for a laugh and a good time, I needed to invest in the ones who were there for *me*. They were the people who would stick around when the music stopped and it wasn't fun any more. They were the people who would walk with me through dark times, and pick me up and encourage me. They were the people who would listen and were worth listening to. They were the people who made me feel whole and loved and surrounded.

When I'm not in that place, and those lonely moments occasionally come, I like to write down how I'm feeling. I listen to myself and put words to the sense of sadness. I ask myself questions about why I'm feeling that way and write the answers down. Then I take the time to think about whether or not the circumstances are within my control or whether I need to adjust my mentality towards them and find acceptance. Sometimes I need to remind myself that I am loved and not lonely, and then force myself to pick up the phone to someone like Briony, even if I don't feel like it.

These days I love my own company, and will deliberately take time to rest and recharge alone. That doesn't make me lonely. I find it gives me the space to appreciate myself, and having quality 'me time' also allows me to enjoy the time I spend with the people I love so much more. I enter those days feeling refreshed and excited to give them all my attention, because I'm no longer spreading myself so thin.

23
The clean-up operation

The doctor who designed the cryosurgery, Dr Nimrod, flew over from the Middle East to perform the surgery on me. I was pleased to be in the hands of Dr Nimrod and other experts, but I was still terrified. I had never been placed under general anaesthetic before, and I was aware that there were risks. Even if the surgery went well, I didn't have a clue what the future would look like on the other side of that operating theatre. The doctors warned me that the recovery process would take a while and would be painful, but that didn't help me to prepare. As it was such a new treatment, and they were using me as a case study, even they weren't exactly sure what would happen next.

The surgery was scheduled for the end of March 2019, almost a year to the day of my accident in Chicago. The night before, I got a total of forty minutes' sleep. In the morning I packed a bag and my mum drove me and my close friend Amir to St Helens Hospital in Merseyside. I was so nervous I couldn't think straight enough to decide what to take with me, so I left Mum sitting outside in the car waiting for a while. She was angry that I hadn't been better prepared, and we had a blazing row on the way there. Looking back, I think we were both scared and stressed, which made us snappy with each other. We always take our worst feelings out on those we love most.

Amir and my mum stayed by my side the entire time. Amir is a talented film-maker, and we agreed that he would document the process so I could show others a snippet of my journey. I watch those videos back now and I can hear myself sounding conflicted. I was happy that I was finally making progress, having waited a long time for this treatment. But I can also see from the footage that I was scared. I look tired, and I can see the dread in my eyes.

I was in theatre under general anaesthetic for four hours. During this time, they injected liquid nitrogen into the tumour in a series of punctures along my chin and neck. When I came round, I remember feeling as though I couldn't breathe. There was a searing pain in my neck, and my throat felt all but closed up. I was panicked at first, but the nurses soothed me and helped me to regulate my breathing.

I was transferred to to nearby Whiston Hospital, as St Helens didn't have the facilities for people to stay overnight. Amir filmed me again when we arrived there. I was drowsy from the medication and all wrapped up, with heavy, blood-soaked bandages around my neck. I couldn't believe the amount of pain I was in, but I felt pleased that it was done, and that the procedure had gone according to plan. I had felt controlled by the scar for a full year by this point, and I just wanted to reclaim my life. I thought I was finally getting there.

I had to stay in hospital for a week, but this time it was different. I had a lot of visitors, and my family were there by my side every day. One friend, Will, even got a cab to the hospital from Manchester. When he got there, he placed a mammoth Domino's order and we chowed down on pizza, all the sides, a massive pot of garlic-and-herb dip and a tub of Ben & Jerry's. Once we'd finished stuffing our faces, he 'borrowed' a wheelchair from the hallway and pushed me around the floor my room was on, desperately trying to avoid any medical staff who would inevitably have told me to get back to bed.

I knew my friends were shocked by my appearance after the operation and by the way my scar looked. It quickly ballooned, so that it was even bigger and redder on the side of my face. As the bloody liquid drained from inside the tumour over the next few days, I had to have absorbent sheets placed on my neck to soak it all up. These were the same pads you might use for a new puppy or a child who wets the bed. The bandages became sodden so quickly that they had to be changed every couple of hours. I took a selfie with the chunky dressing covering my neck and sent it to my girls' WhatsApp group, asking why I was wrapped up like a gammon leg at Christmas!

The healing process was slow, and I needed a lot of care, so I moved back in with my parents for a while. For the first couple of weeks, I didn't spend much time out of bed. My bedroom at home looked like a florist's shop with the number of flowers that arrived from friends, and even from brands that had heard about my story on social media. The process of changing my bandages was lengthy, and it had to happen often. I couldn't move my neck for a long time, and rather than face the challenge of getting dressed, I stayed in my PJs with my hair in a messy bun on the top of my head.

As I grew stronger, I rejoined the wider world and started going to events again. I was regularly posting about my recovery on social media, and I felt proud to be able to go to parties with a face full of makeup and my neck fully bandaged. There was something empowering about owning the injury and recovery so boldly for everyone to see.

The tumour itself started to change rapidly. As the initial swelling went down and the liquid drained, it turned a yellowy brown colour as it started to dry out. The edges began to peel away from my skin, and it was like a nasty scab that was angry and taking time to heal – only far, far bigger. In time this changed again. It turned black in the middle, with a green tinge around the edges, almost like the colour of mould on cheese. And finally, it completely dried out until, one day in the shower, a huge chunk just fell off.

I looked down at the slug-like lump of skin swirling around in the water. I immediately got out of the shower and called my mum: 'Mum, my face just fell off in the shower. What do I do?'

I'll be honest, she was as stumped as I was. I know mums know everything, but this was uncharted territory, even for her. I picked it up, but didn't have the heart to throw it in the bin. So I found a small Tupperware box to put it in before popping it in the freezer. And it is sitll sitting there next to my peas, like it's no big deal.

24
Another one bites the dust

After the operation, the doctors waited months to decide what action to take next. They wanted to see how the skin responded and how it was healing. After allowing some time for it to settle, they concluded that there was enough of the tumour left to warrant doing the procedure one more time to remove more of the protruding skin. It wasn't the outcome I wanted, but I was happy to follow the doctors' lead if it meant that the scar would finally be flat.

The second time around I didn't feel quite as scared because I wasn't facing the unknown. Having completed the process once before, I at least knew how to prepare myself. The surgery itself wasn't a concern; I was just worried that I would go stir crazy sitting in bed for weeks on end again. But I'd had a lot of time to reflect the last time, and had done a lot of growing up.

The initial accident was hard to deal with, but the uphill battle to get my life back on track was making me wiser and stronger. As I spoke out on social media about how I was feeling and the treatment I was having, I received more and more messages from others who were dealing with something big. I knew I needed to get through the second operation so I could get well and start helping people. I was ready to close the book on this chapter and welcome in the next.

When I woke up from the second operation, I felt more emotional than I had the first time. It all caught up with me, and the prospect of getting through the next few months was weighing heavily on my mind. The severe pain was back, and once again I had to fight to breathe. It felt as if someone had slit my throat.

I was prescribed medication to ease the pain, but within a few days the analgesics were downgraded. When the doctor came to do his rounds, I explained the amount of pain I was in and asked for more of the strong stuff. He became very dismissive and told me I should be 'feeling better than this', in an accusatory tone. I couldn't tell whether he thought I was being dramatic, couldn't handle the pain, just wanted more of the drugs, or that it was my fault my body hadn't healed as he had expected. Whatever the reason, I was unimpressed. I know that doctors are the experts, but I wasn't expecting my pain to be so bluntly disregarded.

Once he had left, I called the nurse and told her I didn't want to be seen by that doctor the next day, or any day after that. After a long chat with her, I got the impression a lot of people found him difficult, and I felt pleased that I'd stood up for myself. It's hard to advocate for yourself when you're in a vulnerable position after an operation.

This time round I had to stay on the cancer ward at Whiston Hospital, as they didn't have a private room available. My bed was across the room from an octogenarian called May. She was forgetful, and every morning she would wake up disorientated. As soon as I saw her stir, I would shout over: 'Morning, May!' to help her remember who and where she was.

She always read the papers first thing, then we ate breakfast together. She told me her husband had been a sailor, and he had also sustained a serious burn while he was working. He had sadly passed away, but she reminisced for hours about the boat trips he had taken her on around Sweden and Norway. May told me she used to sneak out of the house after her 8 p.m. curfew while they were 'courting' to go dancing with him. Their song was 'Love Bug' by George Jones, so I would put it on my phone, and then we would shuffle around to it on the ward.

Being in hospital in the UK felt nothing like it had in Chicago. This time I knew I had my friends and family beside me. My friends Ellie and Joss drove over to see me, and they brought a 'get well soon' Build-A-Bear with its own wheelchair. My mum and dad came by regularly, and so did my brother and sister.

When it was time to leave, I decided to go back to my own flat rather than stay with my parents. The process of changing the bandages was second nature to me by that point, so I felt confident that I would be all right looking after myself. I had lots of visits from my family, including cousins, so I didn't feel any sense of isolation.

I dreaded having to shower, as getting the wound wet caused it to sting intensely. I was prescribed strong medication to help me cope with the pain, so once again I spent a lot of time in bed, knocked out by the painkillers. As the days wore on, I started to get impatient to see my skin healed. I wanted to know what my face would look like after all this treatment.

Once I had made enough progress for a doctor to take another look, I went to see Charlotte, who was delighted with the way it was healing. She said I would have to start having steroid injections in order to promote the growth of the new healthy cells, but that sounded like nothing compared to full-on surgery. There were still some areas where my skin was lumpy, but the injections were supposed to help rectify that.

When she administered the first injection, I was in agony. Neither of us had realised the scar was so solid that the needle wouldn't be able to pierce it. Even when she put some real welly into it, the syringe just couldn't get through the thick layer of tissue on the surface.

Charlotte did eventually manage to administer the liquid, and I returned for regular top-ups. After a while she told me that in order to prevent the tumour from growing again, they wanted to do chemo injections. These would affect so much more than the scar. They would make me feel nauseous and exhausted, and would cause my hair to thin.

I was also sent to have a new compression mask fitted. In some ways this felt like a step back, like we had come full circle, as that had been the first treatment we tried after the accident. But in reality it wasn't, because this time it was the right way forward to treat the remaining scar tissue.

The healing process has been slow, and even now, four years later, my scar is still changing. I'm careful to apply creams to it regularly, and still have regular check-ups at the hospital. As I write this at the end of 2023, I've only recently been told that I no longer need the chemo injections. Hearing this was an enormous relief after the difficult side effects I had experienced.

It's been a tough journey, but I'm proud that I stuck with it.

25
Wearing my scars

We've all got scars. I wear mine on my skin, and they're visible even when I wear foundation. Yours may be on your leg, your back, or somewhere that is always covered up by your clothes. Or they may be buried deeper, in your mind. No one gets away with a pain-free life, and pain leaves scars.

I cried over mine for a long time. I wished them away. I experimented with ways to camouflage them or Photoshop them out of my life. I thought people would judge me. I thought I wasn't as pretty or sexy as other women with perfect skin. I felt worthless and embarrassed. But now I see things differently. I wear my scars with pride.

My scars aren't just the marks of an accident that happened when I was twenty-two. Ingrained within them are some of the most important lessons I've learned in my life. They have taught me to be strong. They have taught me that I am so much more than my looks. They have taught me to persevere. They have taught me humility. They have shown me that I have friends who will never judge me for my skin, but who love me for my heart.

I feel liberated when I display the marks on my face at events or online, because it challenges what other people see as beautiful. It gives visibility to something the world tells us to hide away. I feel stronger when I show myself: all of me. My scar is an important part of that. I'm done hiding who I am. I'm done hiding the vulnerability. I'm done hiding the imperfections. I love every part of me, and I'm proud to show myself as I really am.

26
Speaking out

I had dabbled in the influencer world before the accident. I would post the occasional video of me dancing or fire-breathing. But it wasn't until I started showing the rawest parts of my life that my following began to grow. I love to post about the fun and glitzy parties, and to show off my favourite outfits, but I also know it's important to be real about where I'm at. I posted pictures of me in my hospital bed. At points I even opened up in conversations about my mental health. It felt like uncharted and uncomfortable territory for me, but I wanted to be open about my decision to speak to a counsellor.

After posting my first vulnerable video, where I removed my makeup and revealed my scar on camera, I felt sick. But going back to it a couple of hours later, I saw that the comments section was inundated with kind and encouraging messages. It felt like a relief that I was being accepted and embraced. It was even more encouraging when I started to receive messages from people who felt inspired to be more courageous in displaying their own scars after seeing me reveal mine. I was proud to speak out for people who hadn't previously felt they could do so for themselves.

Posting that video was a huge leap of faith. In recent years, authenticity and showing the messy side of your life has become a big feature on social media. But in 2018, when I started doing it, most people were still only showing the highlights reel of glam shots and filtered photos. It was nerve-wracking, but it allowed me to be in charge of the narrative in a way that made me feel empowered. No one could catch me out or laugh at me, or tell people about my scars – I had already owned them. There was nothing left for them to say.

Other people started sharing my posts, and some ended up going viral. I received a message from writer, TV presenter and fellow burns survivor Katie Piper on Instagram telling me I was going to be OK. *Dragons' Den* investor and *Diary of a CEO* podcaster Steven Bartlett shared a link to my page and said: 'This girl is an inspiration to me, go read her story.' TV presenter and DJ Maya Jama even liked a few of my posts, which almost made me burst, as she's my biggest girl crush. It was a bit overwhelming to feel supported by people I respected so much. It made me feel that I wasn't alone, and that I was representing others well.

The internet is, however, still the internet. Despite ninety-nine per cent of the messages I receive being positive, there's still that one per cent. And as much as I try to brush the nasty comments off, I'd be lying if I said they never play on my mind. I get people commenting on my looks and on my scar. I've had people say things like: 'Halloween's come early' and 'Here's Freddy Krueger'.

A few months ago, a huge online media outlet posted my story up for its 14 million followers. Some commenters responded with vicious remarks. They said I deserved to die, that I was an awful role model for children and that I'd got what I deserved for playing with fire. Those messages hurt. It's hard to rise above insults that are so personal and go for your character. As time's gone on, I've found myself becoming more resilient to that kind of trolling. I feel sorry for people who get a thrill out of being rude to someone they have never met. It must be such an empty existence if that's how they are choosing to fill it. This doesn't mean that it no longer hurts, but I try to remind myself that most of the comments are there to get a reaction from me. I don't give them the satisfaction. I'm far too busy enjoying my life and spending time with people who see the real me, scars and all.

The truth is, I am a role model now. I can't be held up as an example of someone who made the right choice on every occasion. Instead, I'm someone who got it wrong and was badly burnt, but who has made something beautiful out of the ashes. Much like the name of my character Phoenix in *Grow Your Own*, I have risen up from the flames. I would rather people took the example of those like me who can show them how to pick themselves up after a mistake, deal with the consequences and use it for the good of others, than listen to those who have never got it wrong.

27

Work, work, work, work, work, work

The mainstream media soon got wind of my story from my Instagram posts and started approaching me to share my story. While it wasn't paid work, I was excited to have the opportunity to discuss some of my challenges, and hoped to make a career out of advocacy in the future.

The first interview I gave was to confidentials.com after one of my Instagram posts gained traction. A message slid into my DMs, asking if I would be interested in giving the site an interview. I was excited by the prospect, but I hadn't spoken to the press before. I'm sure I was still experiencing PTSD when I spoke to the reporter, although I didn't recognise that at the time.

The reporter was kind, and the write-up was a good reflection of my story, but I still felt raw speaking about it. I felt apprehensive knowing it would be out there for everyone to read. Answering the questions, and running through the horrific day of the accident and months of treatment afterwards, put me on edge. It's hard to discuss your triggers when they're actively triggering you. The response was overwhelmingly positive when the article came out, so I decided not to hide away, but to keep taking up these opportunities.

The next one was a biggie. I could hardly believe it when a journalist from *Glamour* reached out to ask if I would take part in the magazine's #BlendOutBullying campaign. *Glamour* was one of the magazines I was obsessed with, growing up, so to be invited to feature was a 'pinch me' moment. I got the train to London and went into a studio to film with them. In the short clip, I had to write some of the disgusting words I'd been called by bullies on my face in eyeliner. I wrote 'Chink' on my forehead and 'slit eyes' across my cheeks. I explained that these hurtful words had made me feel embarrassed to be Chinese.

Then they asked me to blend the words with foundation and remove them from my face. As I did so, I said: 'I don't think we should fight bad energy with bad energy. If you're going to reply back, do it with kindness. And if anything, it'll make them think twice.'

I was so proud of the campaign and my contribution to it. Previously, I would never have dreamed of featuring in a magazine like *Glamour* unless I looked my absolute best, but being there, talking about my pain and showing my scar at the same time, was a powerful experience for me.

People who knew me well were shocked when they watched the clip. A lot of friends I'd met as an adult had no idea I'd been spoken to like that in the past. But they could see that I was determined to make an impact and change things for the better. This was the start of showing people the new me; the one who was going to make a difference.

The next media outlet that approached me for an interview was one of the biggest regional newspapers in the UK. I agreed to do the article and spoke to their reporter at length about the accident and the impact it had had on my life. At one point we talked about how it had changed my looks, and how my outlook on life and physical beauty had changed so much. I told them it might have been the best thing that ever happened to me because of the personal growth that had come from the challenges.

The following day my interview went up online, and I googled myself to find it. Sure enough, there I was. They had used a picture of me striking a strong pose with a full glam face of makeup, a glitzy dress and bandages covering my chin and neck. The headline read: 'Manchester firebreather Sophie Lee who set her own face alight says it's the best thing that ever happened to her.' I couldn't believe it. The article made it sound as if I was encouraging others to do the same; that I thought being burnt was trivial or something to be admired.

The article had been posted on Facebook, and was racking up comments from disgusted readers who hadn't read the article but assumed I had deliberately set myself on fire. The clickbait had worked, because it certainly attracted people's attention. But I started receiving death threats from trolls who assumed I was careless and stupid.

I got on the phone to the reporter immediately and told her I was furious about how I had been quoted out of context. I told her that if she didn't take the article down immediately, I would contact a lawyer because the response was having a hugely negative impact on my mental health.

She came back to me and said that as the page had already gone live, there was no way of taking it down. Rather than remove it, which she claimed wasn't an option, they republished the same article with a headline that made the context slightly clearer. It didn't feel like the right solution, but it was the only one I was offered.

That interview provided the most effective media training I could have been given, and I became far more savvy about what I shared with journalists from that point on. I never wanted to open an article and see another headline like that about me.

When *The Sun* approached me to tell my story for its digital women's magazine, *Fabulous*, I was all geared up with my pre-rehearsed story. I had no intention of going off script. This time I was happy with what was written. I felt the journalist had understood the message I wanted to get out there. I hoped people like me would read it and know that there was hope.

Brands started to hear about my story, and it wasn't long before they invited me to take part in their own empowerment campaigns. I posed in a saucy lingerie set for Bluebella's #LoveYourself Valentine's campaign. This helped me to feel feminine, sexy and womanly for the first time since the accident. I'd questioned whether I was still attractive or desirable, but I felt all of those things in that picture. It was part of the process to finding myself again. They captioned the shot with: 'Confident. Grateful. Strong.' I was proud to endorse that message.

Ego Shoes asked me to pose for their Eliminate Girl Hate campaign, which saw me don bright colours and fun footwear with another model. This was the first time a professional artist had done my makeup on a shoot since the accident, and I felt nervous. I was so used to applying it myself. Even though my scar was healing, the burnt areas of skin were still sensitive and needed special care. There have been times on other shoots since this one when I've had to stop a makeup artist and explain how best to apply skincare and foundation, especially if they haven't worked with skin as sensitive as mine in the past. But for this one I didn't, and despite feeling exposed, I liked the end result.

As the offers started to come in, I realised I had to differentiate between the most personal and private parts of my life, and the things I wanted to share publicly. It's difficult when your job is based on your personality, as the lines between the two start to become blurred. I dealt with this by switching on 'Sophie Lee' when I was working. Sophie Lee was no less my personality than Soph – the down-to-earth girl who sits on the sofa and just pulls her hair up into a bun – she was just the aspects of me that I was comfortable having on display. It didn't feel inauthentic to do that; it felt like a wise boundary. When I'm in Sophie Lee mode, I'm full of energy, lots of fun, laughing and joking, but I'm also passionate and speak boldly about my battles. But if you bump into Soph in the street, you're unlikely to get that same level of hype because it's not possible to sustain that all the time. And there's another side of me that likes peace and calm.

It was exciting when I first started connecting with brands and building relationships with them, but it wasn't all smooth sailing. I agreed an endorsement deal with a popular hair care brand. If your Instagram algorithm is anything like mine, you will have seen its adverts. This brand has a moisturising treatment for hair. The team wanted me to show my followers how to apply it and the end results.

I created the video twice and sent it over for them to sign off before I set it live, and both times they batted it back saying it needed to be more shocking. Unsure of what I was doing wrong, I asked if they could be more specific about what they wanted to see.

The brief that came back was jaw-dropping. They suggested that I should make it more shocking by pretending to either cut or burn my hair.

I even went back and clarified that they were asking me to damage my hair in order to work with them. I was disgusted, and immediately explained that I wouldn't be collaborating with them again. I spoke out about what had happened, and a few media outlets published articles about it. The hair care brand released a statement, taking responsibility and apologising for the distress caused. They said: 'This was a complete error of judgement by a new and very junior member of the team and has been dealt with swiftly internally and a full investigation is underway to ensure that this doesn't happen again.'

I never want to be a person who will do anything to make a brand happy and who just wants the payday. I felt disappointed that the company hadn't taken a more personal interest in me when they approached me to work with them. They should have known that the suggestion that I burn myself was wildly inappropriate. It would be for anyone, of course, but it was especially insensitive, given my history.

The campaigns kept flooding in, with Missguided inviting me to take part in their #LoveThySelf female empowerment initiative, which featured a whole load of incredible women. I was so excited to be in the studio with a clothes company I'd been shopping with since I was a teenager. There were always cameras around, constantly filming and snapping us. I later found out that part of the footage was going into a BBC documentary about the brand, which was subsequently released on Netflix. When it came out, friends began calling me to say they had seen me on the show. It felt surreal as things started to snowball.

I told my story again for a LookFantastic campaign about being fearless, and spoke about losing some of my hair when I started the chemo injections for Beauty Works' My Hair Is My Confidence campaign. I was even invited onto BBC News to talk about the ground-breaking treatment I was having to remove the tumour on my face.

It wasn't all emotional declarations and baring my soul, however. I was also invited to be part of a fun advertising campaign for popular Manchester fast-food chain Archie's. I loved their burgers and used to go there with friends all the time. The vibrant posters started popping up all over town, and then suddenly my face, partially covered by a burger, was all over the buses and taxis. After one night out, a friend and I got a ride home in a cab that was covered with my face! Not only that, but the guys who run the Archie's chain gave me a black card that allows me to eat there for free whenever I want!

28
More than work

Some of the most exciting things to have happened in the last couple of years were nothing to do with work. After reaching out to me on social media when I was in hospital, Katie Piper and I stayed in touch, messaging every now and again on Instagram.

When I started getting better, I wanted to be involved with the Katie Piper Foundation – her incredible charity, which supports burns survivors and people with scars following traumatic incidents. I had been aware of Katie for years, and was really touched by her kind words when I was at my lowest ebb. I truly think she's one of the greatest women of our time, and the awareness she's brought on behalf of burns survivors is extraordinary. Her strength is an inspiration to me, and I wanted to do something to contribute to the work of her foundation.

I joined the foundation's team for the ASICS 10k run. Running 10k isn't a big deal for some people, but I am not one of those people. I've always danced, and I exercise regularly, but running isn't my thing. Before the race, the only thing I had ever run was a bath!

There were so many people there raising money for charity, and thankfully the atmosphere was one of genuine encouragement for runners at all levels. Katie was also running, and this was the first time I had met her in person. The mood was truly electric.

A whole bunch of us ran together, and I'll never forget what happened when we approached a drinks station with rows of plastic cups ready for people to grab on the go. Katie grabbed one of the cups and threw its contents over her face to cool herself down, only to realise that it wasn't water. It was Lucozade! The orange liquid made her face and top sticky, so she had to seek out a water stand and dowse herself down to clean it off. We had a big laugh about it. It's good to know that the people you look up to make mistakes too!

I finished the race in one hour, ten minutes and forty-four seconds. I certainly didn't break any world records, but I was proud of myself. I crossed the finish line, then went straight off to one side and laid down on the floor to get my breath back. It was my first and only sponsored run, but it was all worth it for the team experience and the money we raised.

Rewards and awards

It wasn't long after that I started to be nominated for awards. I was shortlisted for prizes like 'Mental Health Influencer of the Year', by PrettyLittleThing (PLT), and I was invited to give a speech and hand out a prize at the Recognition of Excellence Awards 2022. In 2023, I was nominated for the year's 'Woman of Honour'. The award ceremony was held at the Royal Armouries Museum in Leeds – the same location as the infamous Heely-gate incident from back when I was winding my teachers up at school.

Just being there felt surreal. It was one of the places where I'd been so badly behaved, and it felt like the setting for my unruly teenage years. I looked around and breathed it all in. I could see how far I'd come. My life flashed before my eyes – but not because I was dying, like in a film, but because I was living. Really living.

I had brought my mum to the ceremony, and I could have cried when I won the award. I was handed an official-looking glass award with 'Woman of Honour, Sophie Lee' etched onto it.

I took the award with me the next time I went to my parents' house. My dad slowly surveyed it, reading the writing on the front. 'Very nice, very nice,' he said. Then he put it down on the side.

My father is a man of few words, but I knew he was beaming with pride inside. In Chinese culture, honour is one of the most sought-after attributes. I suppose people who have watched *Mulan* will have picked up on that. It's the same in our family.

Dishonouring your parents is a terrible thing to do, but bringing honour to your family is the highest commendation. I joked that I had now done my job as a good Asian daughter, and I could pack up and go home to bed! It felt like a special moment for all of us.

29
Burnout

Working hard has always been important to me. Achieving my goals has always been non-negotiable. But I started becoming really hard on myself if I ever fell short of perfection. I didn't want to pass up any opportunity, for fear that it wouldn't come around again and I would have missed out. I prioritised taking on new projects over other things. This left me feeling burnt out and empty.

Don't get me wrong, I am proud of every single thing I've achieved. But I had to learn that my worth wasn't limited by the accomplishments I could post on my Instagram grid. I would have been just as valuable as a person without any of it. I once heard someone say, 'If you don't make time for your wellness, you'll be forced to make time for your illness.' This is so true. Allowing time for rest has been especially important for me over the last few years as I've been trying to get better, both physically and mentally.

I realised that if I didn't take some time off, and I mean real time off, when I wasn't constantly available on my phone or by email, I would end up completely drained. I would stop doing things well and start just getting by, and that's no good for anyone.

There were full days when I felt so overwhelmed and rundown that I would cancel everything and just stay in bed. I stopped feeling grateful and started feeling stressed by every offer that came my way. I wanted to help others and get my message out there, but I realised I couldn't pour from an empty cup. If I didn't top myself up, I would have nothing to give anyone else.

These days, I allow myself to feel what I'm feeling. When overwhelm or exhaustion start to creep in, I've learned that it's not my cue to plough on, but to slow down and look after myself. Sometimes that means a night out with my friends, sometimes it means a night in with the lovely Ben & Jerry (my other trusty friends). Whatever will feed me and make me feel most 'held' in the moment, that's what I allow myself to do. I now know that those feelings are temporary. By allowing myself to recharge and regroup, I actually speed up the process of releasing the negativity. Then I can venture back into work or other projects feeling stronger and more on top of my game.

30
Back to school

I was first approached about sharing my experiences in schools by the Leeds United Foundation. The charity funds initiatives in the area, one of which is the Positive Choices Programme, where people with impactful stories go and speak to young people. I am one of many people who have taken part. The foundation also invites recovering drug addicts, people who have served time in prison, stab victims and former drug dealers to share their hard-learned lessons. I have often been in awe listening to these testimonies.

I signed up to go and encourage the next generation, and was sent straight into one of the roughest schools in Leeds. These young people weren't going to listen quietly as I imparted my wisdom. They were completely wired! I watched them messing about, and wondered whether I was there to get a taste of my own medicine. Was I really this bad when I was younger? Probably, yes.

I gave the talk that I am now so familiar with sharing. I start by introducing myself, then tell the story of my time at school, the accident, my treatment and the lessons I've learned through it all. Rather than just speaking about myself, I try to make the session relevant to these young people and where they are at in their lives. I put a picture of myself, wrapped in bandages and looking vulnerable, up on the screen and ask the teens: 'Would you say anything mean to that girl?' Without fail, they reply with a resounding 'No!' (Although they aren't likely to admit it to me, even if they would have). Then I flip it round and explain that they shouldn't be saying anything mean to someone in the corridor either. Just because they can't see that the other person is in pain, doesn't mean they aren't. Just because their scars aren't visible, it doesn't mean they're not there. I also take the opportunity to talk about race, speaking out against the horrible treatment I was subjected to when I was in school. I try to say the things about acceptance that I would have wanted to hear as a young girl of thirteen or fourteen.

I happily tell the naughtier kids that I was just like them, and I'll be real with them about where that behaviour can lead. I explain that I know now that I acted up and became the class clown because I was insecure. I was trying to be liked in all the wrong ways and for all the wrong things. I'm aware that most of the pupils will never experience something as serious as I have, and I'm grateful for that. But I want them to benefit from the lessons I have learned without having to live them out themselves.

31

The fire within

When it comes to inner strength, I get mine from a number of places. I'm comforted when I think about everything I've lived through. It reassures me that I'm made of tough stuff. If I've made it this far, there's nothing that can break me.

I take strength from the love of my friends and family. I know that even on my worst days, they will always cheer me on. Having this safety net, provided by the people who know me best and love me most, makes me feel much stronger than I would if I had to face the world alone.

I believe in God, too. I think back to the timing of the accident on Easter Sunday, the day Jesus was resurrected to new life, and wonder if that was destined to be the day that I entered into my own new life. I like the idea that we're all God's children, and I believe he gives us strength, as well as the ability to love and the ability to forgive. I believe it's up to us to choose whether we want to do those things. I don't feel angry at God for what happened, or that it's his fault. What I do see is that he has been with me through the darkest times and helped me to come out the other side a better person. I've felt guilty for not always behaving well. I'm not proud of the way I've spoken about myself in the past. Psalm 139:14 in the Bible says that we are 'fearfully and wonderfully made', and by being rude about myself, I feel I've insulted God's creation.

It's been a challenge, both mentally and physically, but I feel strong now. To me, strength is being able to stay true to yourself, no matter what or who would try to sway you off course. No one can prepare themselves for the tests that will come in life. We only get to test our strength when difficulties arrive. I believe that we can all step up and find that inner strength when it counts.

32
These days

These days, I feel safe just being me. I'm free to be the daughter of Chinese immigrants, the devoted granddaughter, the kite flyer, the sister, the dancer, the victim of bullying, the class clown, the actor, the friend, the fire-breather, the patient, the survivor, the believer, the activist, the advocate, the party girl, the influencer and the public speaker. I am Sophie Lee, who speaks out, and Soph, who curls up on the sofa. None of these parts of me contradict the others; I am allowed to coexist in all these states. I'm proud of each aspect because I can see that they were all vital steps in the road that has taken me to where I am today.

These days, I've learned to love my body, scars and all. I only get one, and I'm going to treat it well. I have nothing to strive for and nothing to prove. I do my best to nourish my body with what it needs, and I love experimenting with my dad's recipes – although he'd kill me if he knew that I made stirfry in a pan instead of a wok. I still treat myself by inviting Ben & Jerry over every now and again. I marvel at what my body can do; the way it can move and bend and flex. The way it can regenerate and heal. I rest when my body tells me to and push myself when I know the discipline will do me good.

These days, I'm excited about every opportunity that comes my way. I'm surrounded by people who inspire me, and I aspire to do the same for others. I want to keep investing in people and quietly plug away at my goals. I am honoured to speak in schools and to be able to tell my story. I've even released a book (maybe you've already heard about it!). And I'm open to where life takes me next.

These days, I'm dating. And even if I'm not going to spill all the tea, you can rest assured that I am not settling for anything less than I am worth. I strive to be a good teammate to anyone I'm in relationship with, whether romantic or otherwise. I know that popularity is overrated, but kindness and integrity are to be prized.

These days, my family and I are closer than ever. We talk when things are tough and have learned to forgive quickly. I look forward to family nights out even more than those with my friends. I will never be happier than when I'm on a dance floor with my mum, laughing with my brother, singing karaoke with my dad or making TikTok videos with my sister. I treasure all of these moments.

These days, I won't be beaten. I will not be consumed by the fire. I will always rise from the ashes, like a phoenix. I will set the world alight, and I will allow myself to burn brightly. I will love myself, because I am fearfully and wonderfully made. I am finally comfortable exactly as I am.

In my skin.

Acknowledgements

I didn't take the opportunity to write this book lightly, and I am so grateful to the many people who have helped me get here.

Of course, I want to say thank you to my family. My mum and dad, who sacrificed so much to give us all the opportunities they didn't have. My grandma and grandpa for every happy moment from my early years. My brother Kelvin and sister Shivie, who are not just my family but also amazing friends to me. You all believed in me and loved me when I was hard to love, and for that I thank you with all my heart.

My art teacher Mrs Arkwright, who helped me see the beauty in creativity, and my dance teacher Lucy, who always cheered for me and encouraged me to pursue my dreams.

Thanks to Briony for always being a true friend, and to Amir Shah, Alex Khan, Daisey and Ellie O'Donnell, Jay Hill and Lucinda Ashworth, who always have my back. And every single brand that has booked me to work with them and every media outlet that has allowed me to spread my message of hope.

It goes without saying that I owe my life to the skilled medical professionals who cared for me and offered me such cutting-edge treatment. Thank you especially to Charlotte Defty and Dr Nimrod, without whom I wouldn't have the life I do now.

Next, I would love to thank Katie Piper for seeing something in my story that was worth sharing with the world, and for being such a supportive friend and an inspiration. Thanks to everyone in Katie's team who cheered me on. I'd also like to say thank you to all the people at SPCK publishing house: Elizabeth Neep and Wendy Grisham, my editors; Lauren Windle, my editorial consultant; and all the editorial, design and marketing teams who helped make this book what it is.

Acknowledgements

And finally, to you. Yes, you holding this book! Thank you for coming on the journey with me. Let's all agree to stay grateful, humble and kind. I will if you will.

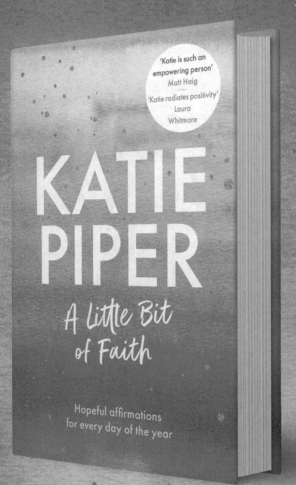

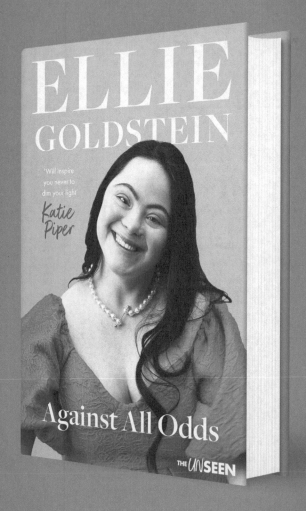